MEMOIRES
of
JAPAN 1946

(A PEOPLE BOWED BUT NOT BROKEN)

BERNARD T. SMITH

Order this book online at www.trafford.com
or email orders@trafford.com

Most Trafford titles are also available at major online book retailers.

© Copyright 2012 Bernard T. Smith.

All rights reserved. No part of this publication may be reproduced, stored in a retrieval system, or transmitted, in any form or by any means, electronic, mechanical, photocopying, recording, or otherwise, without the written prior permission of the author.

Printed in the United States of America.

ISBN: 978-1-4669-6309-2 (sc)
ISBN: 978-1-4669-6311-5 (hc)
ISBN: 978-1-4669-6310-8 (e)

Library of Congress Control Number: 2012919168

Trafford rev. 10/16/2012

 www.trafford.com

North America & international
toll-free: 1 888 232 4444 (USA & Canada)
phone: 250 383 6864 ♦ fax: 812 355 4082

Dedication

I should like to dedicate all my writings of 1946 to all those wonderful colleagues and Japanese friends who in 1946 were in Japan and who are mentioned in my book. Many are sadly no longer with us to appreciate my belated reminiscences, and the enormous gratitude which I felt, and still do feel, for all the help and guidance which they gave me during a very formative time in my life. Hopefully some of their descendants, and others who knew these precious friends of mine, may one day get to know about the traumatic experiences which so many of us shared during that tragic and immediate post war period.

On a more personal note, I should like to thank most gratefully my niece, Dr Janet Wyatt, for so patiently reading, re-reading and improving, another of my books. This is the very same Janet to whom I have referred in the last paragraph of Chapter 1. I should also like to thank, Mr. Colin Wyatt, her husband, for repairing and brilliantly bringing to life again, some very old photographs and an amusing newspaper cutting of the time, by using today's modern digital technology. They are truly a valuable testimony to the validity of the text.

Bernard Smith,
Ealing, London.

October 2012

Preface

(A Strange Lapse Of Time)

That I should have felt compelled to write my account of Japan 1946, now so many years hence, when we are all getting older and our memories are becoming fainter, is a strange event and deserves an explanation.

In 2011, I had the good fortune to read again Air Vice Marshal Bouchier's excellent autobiography*, "Spitfires In Japan". I was tempted to look through all my old collection of records, documents, and photos, which I had not looked at for years; and, to my utter amazement, I found three months of a 1946 diary which I had kept at the time, and also 166 pages of foolscap hand written notes of my time in Japan, which I had written aboard the ship which subsequently brought me home in that very same year.

At the time when I wrote about these events they were very fresh in my mind. Now, in the year 2012, it means that, although we have moved on so very many years, I am still able to make a useful contribution to the history of that time. My book is very much about human suffering and personal experiences as opposed to say formal Government publications and impersonal reports. I discussed the situation in one of the discussion groups at the U.K. Japan Society 2011 AGM, which was held at the Japanese Embassy in June of that

Memoires of Japan 1946

year, and I was strongly urged to have a shot at writing what I have now called, as above, "Memoires of Japan 1946 (A People Bowed But Not Broken). It attempts to show the utter shock and desolation which the Japanese were feeling at the beginning of 1946 and the remarkable resilience with which they began to recover in that same year.

Except for Chapter 25, about my unexpected and somewhat mystifying visit to Tokyo in June or July 1946 (when I have had to rely mostly on my memory) my book is dependent entirely on the notes which I made while travelling home from Japan at the end of my tour of duty. There was a slot in my notes for this rather mysterious "mission" to Tokyo but I didn't get round to writing about it. If a Japanese name or phrase quoted in my book is incorrect, due either to a mistake in my notes or later in my faulty memory, I do most sincerely apologise to my readers. Needless to say that, without my precious notes, the present book would almost certainly never have been written. I am more than grateful that fate has, after all, eventually intervened and decreed that these very remarkable events in my life need not be forgotten.

Bernard Smith,
London

* Published by Global Oriental

Contents

Part I: From The Very Beginning

Chapter 1:	Kicking Our Heels………………………………………………	3
Chapter 2:	Bombay to Japan ………………………………………………	8

Part II: Seven Months of Wonder

Chapter 3:	Arrival in Japan …………………………………………………	15
Chapter 4:	Chain of Command ……………………………………………	22
Chapter 5:	The Early days…………………………………………………	26
Chapter 6:	The Namiwaki's—A Glimpse of Family Life ……………	33
Chapter 7:	Daily Routine at the Camp ………………………………	36
Chapter 8:	Appreciation From Girls at the Camp ……………………	43
Chapter 9:	Party-Going and the Story of A Geisha …………………	47
Chapter 10:	Happy Days with the Namiwaki's ………………………	53
Chapter 11:	Changing Times ………………………………………………	58
Chapter 12:	The local Police Chief ………………………………………	62
Chapter 13:	AMG Liaison Officer …………………………………………	67
Chapter 14:	The Mayor ……………………………………………………	69
Chapter 15:	The City Headmaster ………………………………………	73
Chapter 16:	The Miyazaki's—Another Wonderful Family! …………	78
	Restored images of the Time…………………………	88-102
Chapter 17:	Good Bye To Jock and The End of an Era ……………	103
Chapter 18:	Walkabouts in Iwakuni ……………………………………	107
Chapter 19:	The Iwakuni Cultural Society ……………………………	114
Chapter 20:	Contact with the Miyazaki's is Resumed………………	123
Chapter 21:	Visit to the Local Mrs Vanderbilt and My First Tea Ceremony……………………………………………	130
Chapter 22:	The Cultural Society and Humour………………………	139
Chapter 23:	The Cultural Society and The Status of Women ……	145

– IX –

Chapter 24:	Talk on the Average British Housewife	149
Chapter 25:	An Unexpected Visit To Tokyo	154
Chapter 26:	With the Miyazaki's at the Pictures	160
Chapter 27:	Final Days and Fond Farewells	167

Part III: Thoughts on a Memorable Experience
(A case of Introspection)

Chapter 28:	A Charmed Existence	175
Chapter 29:	Hard to Believe	180
Chapter 30:	And What Came Next?	184
Appendix A:	Paragraph Headings By Chapter	189
Index		195

PART I

FROM THE VERY BEGINNING

Chapter 1

Kicking Our Heels

Kashmir, India

The date was 15 August 1945, just two days after my 23rd birthday. I was in India, at the end of the Second World War. Peace in South Asia had at last been declared. For me, it was the beginning of the most pensive, edifying, formative, and rewarding period of my life. As a young (and by no means worldly wise) Flight Lieutenant in His Majesty's Royal Air Force, I had been enjoying a holiday in Kashmir having served in both India and Burma over a period of about one and a half years. Celebrations were going on everywhere. At an officers' club dance, I had just been proposed to by an elegant Indian Parsee lady who had promised me "great wealth" if I would only team up with her. At that moment, however, I had other, more serious, matters on my mind; Japan was on the horizon.

Three months in New Delhi

I returned to my base in New Delhi. We were being offered "repat" (repatriation) or, if we preferred, a short tour of duty with the proposed Allied Occupying Force in Japan. I chose the latter at once and was accepted almost immediately, probably because I had some knowledge of Japanese. I had previously spent almost a year on a crash course studying the language at the University of London's, School of Oriental and African Studies (SOAS). But, I never expected that it was going to be nearly another six months or more, before I finally arrived in Japan. I had been very happy both in India and in my unit. Everyone had been very kind to me during my service there. I was very grateful to them for this. At one time, with a small group of other officers, I had even been a guest of the Maharajah of the state of Datia, with its Prime Minister no less being our escort. Whatever could be the reason for the delay in our going to Japan? We had no idea. We had thought it was just slow bureaucracy—our Administration was certainly very busy at the time—but, as we later realised, it may have been more to do with the difficulty of making room for us.

Kindness in India

The kindness I had received in India continued throughout the long following months which were to come. Both India and my unit continued to help me occupy my time gainfully. In order to practise using my Japanese, I was invited to make regular visits to the Red Fort in New Delhi where many Japanese prisoners were housed, pending their return to Japan. On several occasions, my unit provided me with a jeep and a driver and I was able to converse in Japanese with a small group of Japanese POWs. Occasionally, I took them to places of interest in and around New Delhi. We would finish the day with afternoon tea in one of the prestigious restaurants in New Delhi's Connaught Circus, Davicos or Wengers, sometimes much to the surprise and alarm of other customers. The POWs, who came with me, were usually, Lt. Aizawa, together with a sergeant, and one or two other soldiers. Lt. Aizawa, with whom I remained in contact until his death a few years ago, always insisted that he did not want to go back to Japan. He was, as he saw it, in disgrace having lost the war. I managed to influence him otherwise, and eventually he became a very successful Captain of a ship with the Japanese Nippon Yusen Kaisha. I was intensely interested in Japanese people, having met with many, when studying the language at SOAS and, now also when conversing with Japanese POWs. Forgetting the horrors of war for a moment, I had visions of the romantic way of life in Japan, its many hills, valleys, and it's beautiful Inland Sea, a land of colour, of daimyo, samurai and the 47 Ronin, of feudal castles, heroic deeds, and ladies in their pretty kimonos. One of the prisoners in my care at the Red Fort had once said very touchingly that Japanese women were the most beautiful and gentle women on earth. Lafcadio Hearn (Koizumi Yakumo), a famous international writer in the late 19th century, had written more, having eventually married and spent the rest of his life there. All of this was certainly to have a big effect on me when I finally arrived in Japan.

Goodbye from the Red Fort

My visits to the Red Fort helped me to occupy my time gainfully: but, inevitably, time began to drag. We were just kicking our heels. A few people had opted for "repat", and I seemed to be the only person going to Japan. It was not until early in 1946 that I heard I had been posted to a staging post for overseas travel in Madras, presumably I thought because it was the nearest port to Japan in India. I cycled over to the Red Fort in New Delhi with Michael Kerry (who later became Sir Michael Kerry, solicitor to HM Treasury) to say a fond good bye to the Red Fort staff, Major Mackey, Sgt major Slides, and others, as well as to the POWs there with whom I had conversed. I had a last lingering look at New Delhi and then made my preparations to travel. I was the only person scheduled for Madras so I was quite alone in going there. The next day was a day of goodbyes and departures and a fond farewell at a camp where I had been based for most of the last two years; except, that is, for a Xmas 1944/45 spell in Burma. The journey to Madras was a three night train journey, seemingly through the midst of humanity. The train chugged along relentlessly, through 1300 miles of dull, fair, moderate, and sometimes very interesting scenery. However I did rail, possibly a little unfairly, at what "surely only an Indian rail Company" could be guilty of,—dumping its passengers at the end of a 1300 mile journey, at 3 o'clock in the morning, in the middle of a deserted railway station!

Staging Post Madras

At midday on my first day in Madras (Monday 21st January 1946) I arrived at my temporary destination. This was, a large transit camp, with a large officers' Mess, just outside the city. But, alas, there were still more waiting days to come. Time began to drag again. There were inoculations and vaccinations etc. to get over, and morning drills to occupy our time. We were told that we were ambassadors of our country and that we had to brighten ourselves up and be smart—paradoxically it seemed—to impress those whom we had just conquered. Not all of us were in the same draft. That depended on where we had come from and precisely where we were going. Two of my former Burma colleagues, who had first been posted to Saigon and Phnom Penh in Cambodia, came to the camp from the other side of the Brahmaputra. They arrived at the camp about the same time as me, but they went on to Japan separately from me. We explored Madras together. Of one of them, Flt Lt. Mark McLaughlin, was to be with again later in Japan. Richard Mason who wrote the novel, The Wind Cannot Read,— and whom I first met in SOAS, London University, about three years before, was also there. I used to call in the Admin office regularly to find out what was happening, but without much success. The weather fortunately was beautifully warm and perfect. When I returned to my billet I would see many of my near neighbours sunbathing, scantily covered or sometimes completely nude, relaxing and enjoying their time off duty; but I was anxious to be away and on the move. Suddenly, on Monday 28th January 1946, six of us found ourselves moving, not however towards Japan as we had hoped, but in the opposite direction. We were heading for yet another staging post, this time in Bombay on the other side of the Indian continent. This was where I had first arrived in India two years before. In Madras, I had become used to seeing the morning sun as it was rising over the sea. But now, back in Bombay, I used to watch the evening sun as it was setting over the sea. It gave me a strange, almost eerie, sense of awareness of the daily passage of the sun, as it moved from East to West across the huge Indian continent. Each day, it was heading towards Europe; and also, in my case, home.

Staging Post Bombay

Very happily, there was mail from England waiting for me in Bombay, including a piece of lovely christening cake from my 6 months' old niece, Janet. A little prematurely I sent her a lovely little dressing gown. It was the first time I could ever say, "From Uncle Bernard". This is the self same Janet (now Dr Janet) to whom I expressed my very grateful thanks in my dedication. I also met several former New Delhi colleagues there, who were being repatriated and were on their way home. It was good to see again the Gateway of India, the Taj Mahal hotel, and the beach where on my arrival in India I had bathed and become badly sunburned. At last, things were moving, but we still had

Chapter 1: Kicking Our Heels

a few days (very pleasant ones, as it happened) to spend in Bombay. It was not until the Thursday 7th of February 1946 that we went on board the ship that was to take us to our final destination. Before we set sail, our very small Air Force contingent—of which I was part—was visited by the Air Commodore who was to become our senior AOA (Air Officer Administration). He wished us well and told us that we were the first of about 15,000, or more, Air Force personnel, from all over the Commonwealth, who would be going to Japan during the next few months. He had only one very important instruction for us to follow, and that was that none of the personnel who would be joining us should ever be forced "to live under canvas". The implication was that any required accommodation and chattels for our troops would have to be locally "requisitioned". It was the worst of a number of very painful duties I had to undertake, in an otherwise incredibly wonderful year in my life.

Chapter 2

Bombay to Japan

Goodbye Bombay

We set sail for Japan from Bombay on Saturday 9th of February 1946. We were on a large ship with a mixture and large number of passengers. These included Indian and UK service personnel like me, returning Japanese POWs, Government officials, journalists, and diplomats, some of whom had been in detention during the war and some of whom, on their return to Japan, could well be facing trial. During the voyage, I had discussions with a variety of passengers on many different topics. Of my immediate colleagues, nine of us were cramped in a fairly small cabin; but we were very happy just making do. "Making do" seemed to be the rule of the day. We had the run of the deck, the lounge, and various common rooms on the ship for most of the time, so we tended to use our cabin space almost in shifts. It was a grand feeling, especially in the evening, leaning over the ship's rail with a colleague, dreaming and pondering over the day's events, as we looked into the silent ocean beneath us. Sunday was upon us before we knew it; and I enjoyed the first Sunday morning service, singing the hymn "Guide us over the tempestuous sea!" while contrarily at the same time peering out, at as vast and peaceful a sea as one could imagine. We were a floating city in the midst of nowhere. We had various discussions on how to spend the next three weeks. Four of us in our cabin opted for evening games of Bridge but we soon merged with others. I was for instance often in a game with a Group Captain and a Wing Commander, but I didn't know their precise destinations. As far as I knew, I was the only person destined for HQ British Commonwealth AIR (BCAIR) in Iwakuni, although some personnel were going to Iwakuni itself, as distinct from BCAIR HQ. I don't remember volunteering, but it was somehow assumed that I would teach Japanese to those who were interested. I held two one-hour classes each morning, except Sunday. We also had discussions on several days—on how the Japanese would re-act to our presence when we arrived, and how we should behave. Certainly there were some who said they were out for revenge, who sounded bombastic, and self righteous, with rather a lot of thoughtless bravado; but I always tried, not to become involved in these dubious deliberations. It was all hypothetical anyhow. Our reactions would be decided by events. We too had carried out dubious deeds, as we would surely witness in Hiroshima, even though at the time the actions had been deemed essential. I was anxious, despite all the many horrors and atrocities we had heard of, to cultivate friendships and to leave Japan as a friend.

Columbo to Singapore

On Tuesday 12th February we docked at Columbo in Sri Lanka, which was then known as Ceylon. It was a good opportunity to post mail which I had written aboard the ship since leaving Bombay. On Sunday 17th February, after sailing down the Malaccan straits, we docked in Singapore and I was able to send yet more mail from there. While we were in Singapore we were visited by a Squadron leader, liaison officer from Japan whom I came to know later in Japan as Hank. He had come on board to tell our Group Captain that it was OK for him to fly on to Iwakuni, way ahead of the rest of us. Although the liaison officer spoke with an American accent he had an RAF rank, so I assumed he was from the UK liaison office in Tokyo, rather than the American forces stationed there. I suppose t is possible that he was American. Needless to say, the Group Captain was delighted at his good fortune. Our stopover in Singapore, however, was quite brief; so we were prevented from seeing much of the city. We contented ourselves with a stroll along the dockside and at least a peep into the nearby streets, so as to be able to say that at least we had set foot in Singapore. I would have to wait for many months later, when on my return to the UK; I would have another chance to walk round the rest of Singapore. We could see signs in the streets of the Japanese occupation of Singapore now six months ago,—notices like "No Smoking", written in huge Japanese characters on many buildings. There were also Japanese POWs working there—, far more cheerfully, I suspect, than the British POWs who had been there before them, and who had been made to toil so terribly.

The South China Seas

We woke on Tuesday morning 19th February to find that our ship was moving—having set off in the Stream, as it was called, just after dawn. And so, the last stretch began. We moved northwards gradually into colder climes, rougher and choppier seas, new adventures, and hopefully excitingly new experiences. I re-started my classes after a two day break, but already their numbers had diminished. I was wondering if it was such a good idea, after all. I was giving up two valuable hours per day teaching and then there was also the necessary time to find for preparation. Sometimes, I felt quite exhausted; especially when, in the South China seas, we ran into a storm with dark skies overhead. There was an oppressive atmosphere aboard everywhere. We had heard also that it was becoming a very difficult time in Bombay and India, which we had been very lucky to miss. Riots apparently were spreading out all over India. Bombay had been the scene of considerable disorder. There is little doubt that our departure would have been delayed yet again, had we have been there at the time. We may not have ever seen Japan. The Japanese diplomats on board, with whom I occasionally conversed in order to practise my Japanese, had been seen talking to some Indian service personnel and had therefore been confined to their cabins. This was presumably to avoid any disturbance on the ship. Hence, I didn't get another chance to speak with them, or even to say good bye. Our bridge fours continued most evenings with both my partners and my opponents becoming ever more varied—from colleagues and senior officers, to various doctors, and even the very amusing open hearted NAAFI official, who provided additional food and drinks for us. It all made for good friendship. There were many discussions reconstructing the games we had played, and many attempts to apportion blame for how the games had gone but, I was determined to remain friendly and I never took the discussions very seriously. I always refused to play for more than one anna for each hundred points,—really a very paltry sum.

Hong Kong, Taiwan, and beyond

The third Sunday service of our voyage, on 24th February, was in sharp contrast to the previous two. Looking through the windows of the first class lounge I surveyed the changing scene—beyond Hong Kong and Taiwan. Firstly, I remembered the first sights of the Indian coastline in beautifully sunny weather and the sea so calm and still. It seemed as if we had not been afloat at all. Secondly I remembered our approach to Singapore, still in a lovely warm climate and under its true blue skies. But now, they were cold bleak mornings, with rain likely every minute and, what is worse in a storm, the pitch and toss, and sometimes not so playful rolls, of the ship. At meal times, the Captain would eat his food with a smile in his eyes, and with looks of dismay at his crestfallen passengers. We were barely out of the tropics, and we were already out of our summer kits, and wearing Air Force blue. The ship's crew, were also wearing much warmer clothing. Everyone stayed in bed until the very last minute, and then made a mad rush to be in time for breakfast. On Thursday 28th February, we arrived off shore in Japan; and, we had our first glimpse of the intriguing little islands, which are dotted all about in Japan's lovely Inland Sea (the beautiful Seto nai kai). In the evening, we could see Iwakuni's glittering lights through a grim Scottish like mist, while on deck, it had become bitterly cold. But, slowly, we sailed on towards Kure, for our last night aboard ship, looking forward to our final concert, which we had been told would be of a very high standard.

Part II

Seven Months of Wonder

Chapter 3

Arrival in Japan

Historical musings

We arrived offshore at Kure in Honshu, Japan, on Thursday, the 28th February, 1946, and we stayed on board overnight. After a concert, I tried to imagine what could possibly lie ahead. During the last few days in February, we had seen and followed the rugged contours of the lovely Japanese coastline, as we had steamed through the beautiful Inland Sea sprinkled with its many islands, dotted about like pearls in blue water. Waves and white foam seemed to be beating against the knuckles and toes of southern Japan. Here and there, in the far off hills, we could see cheering trails of smoke rising in a cold wintry setting. What magical secrets still lay there? We were about to take a step back in history. This was Japan. What a marvellous end to a long sea trip. In the heart of Japan, I longed to see nature in her most beautiful and simple dress, untouched by modern developers, untouched by human craft, a country of the past, myth and legend, and romantic traditions. This was the land of Amaterasu, the Sun goddess, "from whom all noble sons are descended"; a land where "earth, and sun, and moon, unite in splendid scenic glory". It was the land of eight headed monsters against whom valiant sons of old had fought; of feudal lords and loyal retainers; of strongholds and castles, heroic deeds, honour, valour, and virtue. Today's tales of war and atrocity could not be true. There was another Japan. It would be found in Nature which I knew was very near to the Japanese heart. The sight of land from seaward is in any case always a welcome sight; it is nature's own. The trails of smoke from those pine topped hills beyond were still rising, still sending out these messages; and, as for me, I had come—very privileged indeed, to see if they were true.

Shattered dreams

On Friday the 1st of March, my "dreaming" at first continued. Everything was still a magical experience. Also, during that day, instead of looking at Japanese characters in a book, I began to see Japanese Kanji for real. They were alive. They had come suddenly to life. What I had learned of Japanese writing and kanji were, after all, part of a real, living, language and a part of peoples' lives. Signs which I could see, with meanings like "passengers to the right; vehicles to the left" were sheer joy. The Kanji meant something, and people responded to them. I was overjoyed. I could see Japan with both eyes. Others, not knowing the language, would see it with only one. But then I learned, that even the sweetest dreams may have the rudest awakening; and this can be, even when the dream is having its most effect. Slowly, as we steamed into the harbour that had been Kure, a formidable naval port and pride and joy of wartime Japan, came into view. My fairyland dream faded. My heart sank. We were nearing the jetty and coming face to face with reality. Barren destruction, ruin, skeletons of former glory lay in the middle distance. Masses of twisted iron girders, rusted and useless, pushed their way up into the dull grey atmosphere. Pillars of steel and strength had lost their battle, and now lay broken and tangled, as if to warn the world that all who practice war shall come to this. To look upon such frozen rusted metal and tattered concrete heaps was like grating my fingernails on a rough surface, and the gnashing of my teeth. It was chilling. This was not the scene I had anticipated.

Air Force reception

We had never expected a welcome from the Japanese people, and indeed there was none. But, neither was there any hostility shown towards us. In fact, at no time during my entire stay in Japan did I ever encounter real hostility. The Japanese people took the view, I believe, that fate had ordained their present situation. They didn't ask why it had happened; it was their lot, they wouldn't fight it, they

Chapter 3: Arrival in Japan

would live with it, there was no resistance. Instead, they would suffer it with stoicism and placidly get on with living. It was an example of the Japanese peoples' remarkable resilience to misfortune which I was to witness on many future occasions. However, to return to the present, waiting below on the quayside to greet those of us who were going to Iwakuni, we could see a very small group of Air Force personnel. It was a small party of seemingly very keen and happy young people who, even if they were blue with cold, seemed more than happy to welcome us. My depression disappeared. Our excitement increased, as they answered questions which we threw down to them from the deck, and they told us tales of what was happening. What is life like? Are you meeting the people? Have you made any friends? The reception party was positive and reassuring. I felt I was a pioneer, fresh after a long voyage, and keen beyond words to get down to the soil below, to go exploring. But, again I suffered the ups and downs of my emotions. Suddenly, I would remember that we were no longer in a prosperous country, a thriving port, or a great naval base, which Kure once had been. Unexpectedly, and very quickly, we had now become face to face with reality, and the grim results of a ferocious war. Very soon I was to witness scenes of even greater, utter, devastation.

The harsh reality of Kure

The diplomats aboard our ship disembarked just before us. I did not have a chance to say good bye to any of them. We joined our welcoming party, and headed for the Kure railway station. Life in the city was dormant, almost lifeless, no action, speed, or vitality. It was bitterly cold, Women would go past dressed in so many clothes that they looked as if they were clothed in balls of wool. Many were wearing "mompei", that is padded trousers tied at the ankle. We were told that, during the war, women had been made to wear them. Despite the cold, their footgear consisted of just toe stringed wooden geta, which we could hear going clap, clap, and clap, over the frozen asphalt. In the market, there were piles of old rubbish on the streets presumably left by vendors. I tried speaking Japanese, but with only a modicum of success—hopefully, I thought, because of the vendors' dialect. In fact, my first transaction in Japanese was shamefully black market. I had no Japanese money, I had not eaten for five hours, and I was hungry. So, I traded 10 cigarettes for two or three pounds of oranges. My colleagues enjoyed them as much as I did. Kure's railway station, when we finally got there, seemed to consist of only a few shacks like much of the city. There were odd combinations of railway lines, which had perhaps once run alongside platforms, or which once led into sheds and repair depots, but which now seemed to go nowhere. The scene seemed to be just as the bombs had left it. Officials were wandering around without any expression, and completely unconcerned that we had been waiting on a deserted station for four long hours. We deserved to be laughed at, but the Japanese seemingly had neither the will nor the energy to do so. I remember the train we boarded. It was my first journey in a Japanese train. Our two Service compartments were half empty but what they lacked in numbers was made up in the huge amount of food and rations which were now suddenly available to us. At last our dry rations had arrived, and we must have looked like starving wolves at a feast. We scoffed and gobbled up our food continuously; while, in the adjoining Japanese coaches, people were packed in like sardines. Gaping mouths and little noses of half starved children, pressed hard against the glass of the sliding doors, emitted the only outward sign of life, as the children's breaths condensed on to ice cold window panes. I felt squeamish about it, but there was little I dare do. I had yet to learn my own place in this new and frightening scenario.

Heartbreak in Hiroshima

The journey through Kure, disappointing as it had been, was nothing compared with the shock and horrors which we experienced a little later, as we approached Hiroshima, about 20 miles away and half way to Iwakuni. Peering through the steamed up windows of the train, we were now looking at the gruesome scenes of a devastated city. It was nauseating. Whole areas of the city were shattered and streets were full of rubble where houses and shops had once been. I knew of course that Hiroshima was one of the two atom bombed cities in Japan at the end of the war. I knew that Hiroshima lay between Kure and my present destination, Iwakuni; and I knew that things were bad. But, I had never imagined such utter devastation, vast areas laid to waste. Houses, homes, firms, factories hotels, shops, municipal buildings, parks,—all part of an eastern capital, which had flourished with the best, had simply disappeared, and were completely obliterated. There

Chapter 3: Arrival in Japan

was nothing standing more than two feet high, except perhaps the odd branch of a tree with its bare twigs in a silhouette against a background of ice, snow and sky, still clinging as fast as it could to life. White-grey gravestones, tombs of countless dead, and perhaps here and there half of a stone built archway, disfigured and blackened by fire, now lying on top of the rubble amid shattered pieces of stone. It was all waste, wilderness, and ruin beyond belief. As our train pulled alongside a newly constructed platform in Hiroshima station, we saw lots and lots of children waiting for our train. They were on their way home from school, cap in hand and with satchels on their backs. The girls especially had round ruddy faces, tomato red cheeks, and dimpled chins; jet black hair cut to a fringe over their foreheads. There were hundreds of faces, all so much alike. The teachers of the girls' middle school must have found it difficult to distinguish between them. Little wonder that they all had names in characters on their blazers. These were the children who were about to inherit new Japan. They would remember us as, with their empty stomachs, they looked with amazement into our carriage where we were munching more food than we could possibly want. They would remember our half empty compartment while theirs were cramped, sometimes with passengers standing on the steps of their carriage, or pushed out half way through their carriage windows. It was not a happy situation for an occupying force to be in. I was very conscious of it. A few of us tried to speak to the children and to give them sweets which we happened to have. One little boy's face on receiving half a bar of chocolate was a tonic for sore eyes. His ruddy cheeks reflected heat; while his twinkling eyes and pure white teeth reflected light. Both were inestimable qualities on such a dismal day. The station guard was waving his flag. I gazed again at the dreary scene once more, the sterile wastes, and barren ground. Hiroshima was once to have been our headquarters. How much better I wondered would Iwakuni be. These were my scary thoughts as Hiroshima disappeared beneath the darkening skies on that cold and dull March afternoon. Grotesque and fantastic shapes were in my mind, like Picasso paintings gone wild. They merged into the distance as slowly we drew away from what once had been a thriving city; but my thoughts about those dreadful scenes we had just witnessed were stubborn They did not fade with time.

Hiroshima's indelible imprint

To bring home the shock and horror of Hiroshima even more permanently, I will describe a visit which I happened make to Kure again, a few days later, this time by road in a jeep, and with some accounting staff to accompany me. This visit meant that we would go again through Hiroshima, and it brought me even closer to its utter desolation. We were moving literally to and fro, traversing completely shattered, barren land. The city was a maze of piled up rubble through which we had to make our way as well as we could. There seemed to be so many rivers running through what had been the city of Hiroshima. During our journey along the ruined and parched pathways we seemed to cross every bridge and railway crossing which had survived, or had been temporarily replaced. We must have crossed the same river many times and in different directions. It took us four hours each way to travel the 40 miles. There were rumbles from time to time beneath the stones and debris. It was eerie, but there was no room for ghosts or spirits in what had been Hiroshima. It was not a city for ghosts. It was a large, flat, wasteland. There were no ruins or forsaken buildings left standing, from which ghosts or spirits could jump out and haunt us. Ghosts and spirits would find no shelter here. However, countless thousands of innocent men, women, and children had died here, all killed at one fell stroke, all from one atomic bomb—all at the hands of us, the so called victors. Only by being there on that fateful Monday, 6th August 1945, would we have really known the full extent of the suffering and torture which was experienced that day. Imagination gripped my mind. I couldn't help myself. The terrible tales I had heard, of how more than 200,000 people had died in the most gruesome of ways, kept haunting me. Clothes literally torn from bodies, the shapes and forms of bodies imprinted in rocks, scales of skin peeled from peoples' faces and limbs, bodies turning blue and red as atomic rays destroyed their blood cells. Of those affected, most had sadly perished; but many were maimed for life, hair had started to fall out until the head was completely bald, skin diseases, infections, ulcers and tumours were already prevalent. Who could tell what further radioactive horrors might still be developing to manifest themselves in the years to come? Here was terrible tragedy. Had such dreadful action really been so necessary? In retrospect, it seemed we were entitled to ask the question. In any case, my experience during these first few days in Japan was a very grim reminder of why we were there at all. Later on, the wretched scenes I had witnessed would often creep back into my thoughts, especially when I was called on to carry out some of our more uncomfortable tasks, like taking away from local inhabitants even some of their most cherished possessions. It was a cruel price to ask so many innocent people to pay when they had already suffered so badly. At the back of my mind, I could never forget, "Remember Hiroshima! Do not forget, Hiroshima!", and I didn't; I couldn't. As the months went by, the city was gradually cleared of its dangerous debris, and new buildings began to appear. I was there again on several occasions, sometimes even on foot, but my first impressions were never changed.

Chapter 4

Chain of Command

AMG-BCOF-BCAIR

We had arrived in Iwakuni on the 1st March 1946, more than six months after the end of the war on 15th August 1945. For the first four months of this time, the occupying authority for the whole of Japan had been the AMG (<u>American Military Government</u>). On the first of January 1946, however, responsibility for control of the southern half of main island Honshu (Yamaguchi, Hiroshima, Okayama) and the island of Shikoku was transferred to BCOF (<u>British Commonwealth Occupational Force,</u> with its headquarters in Kure. The first BCOF personnel to go there were a few Australians who arrived early in January 1946. The first Commander in chief of BCOF was an Australian, General Sir John Northcott. The Air component of BCOF was known as BCAIR (<u>British Commonwealth Air</u>). BCAIR headquarters (of which I was a member) was in Iwakuni, about 40 miles to the east of Kure; but, as yet, it was barely operational. Before and during the war, the city had been the base and headquarters of a very prestigious training base of the Japanese Naval Air Marine Corps. When I arrived there on the 1st March, the senior British officer of BCAIR, who had still to arrive in Iwakuni, was Air Vice Marshal (AVM) Sir Cecil Bouchier. He was also deputy to General Northcott. The whole British force (BCOF), including BCAIR was under the supreme command of the United States' General Douglas MacArthur in Tokyo. Unfortunately, we often had a feeling

Chapter 4: Chain of Command

of being in a rather inferior position to the Americans. Our troops were conscious of this, but so too were the Japanese people. As if in sympathy with our plight, they called the railway station at one of the three airfields we inherited, as "Mitajiri,"—the backside of a rice field;—with the suggestion that our three airfields were little more than paddy fields! Very early on, sadly in the same vein, I was shown a parody of The Lord's prayer written by one of our own troops;
:
"Our General who art in Tokyo,
Douglas MacArthur be thy name,
Thy kingdom be off limits to BCOF troops,
Give us this day our daily directive,
And forgive us for trespassing in the US zone,
As we forgive postal for jettisoning our mail.
And lead us not into insanity,
But deliver us from Iwakuni.
For thine is the kingdom,
And thou art almighty,
For the period of occupation".

This very irreverent little verse was, I believed, probably written very much in fun rather than with any feelings of anger or resentment. The Commonwealth effort and goodwill in the war had been no less than that of the Americans. If it was true that the Americans had won the war in the Pacific, then it is certainly no less true that we had at least stopped the war being lost in Burma.

Arrival in Iwakuni
We had been shocked by what we had seen in Kure and Hiroshima but alas, when we arrived in Iwakuni, I am afraid that it didn't seem that the scene was going to be very much better. Iwakuni and its approaches had not been <u>atom bombed</u>, but they still bore all the marks of a savage aerial attack. Dilapidated buildings; windowless, roofless, floorless, homes; burnt and overturned trains beside railway lines; and upturned vehicles, littered the countryside. The coastal view boasted of even more destruction—but this was from the ravages of typhoon and tidal waves. What tragedy yet again. Some of our senior commanders had not for nothing called Japan a land of disaster

and danger. But doggedly we moved on, convinced that we had a worthwhile task ahead—that is, by our behaviour, to earn the respect of those we had beaten, to show the futility of war, and to help restore sanity among the nations of the world. We needed to replace the despair we had felt after Kure and Hiroshima, with fresh hope and aspiration for a brighter and peaceful future for all nations. I was sure that the British Commonwealth would acquit itself well in this and that, at the end of the occupation, Japan would well be on the way to taking its rightful place again in the comity of nations. By its remarkable prosperity, some 20 to 25 years later, it most assuredly had done so. Iwakuni had been described to us as a little fishing village, which most people had never heard of; but which, both before and during the war, had been transformed in importance, by becoming the headquarters of the aforementioned prestigious Cadet Training College for Japanese Naval Air Officers. The city itself, as we could see, was still a quaint little city with lots of narrow crooked streets. There were flimsy dwellings and shops along the main street, either closed or looking as if they had not done business for years, displaying little else but buttons, studs, and perhaps a few radio parts. The people were mainly peasants, earning their living from the land or the sea, but with a few also owning shops, to make a little money on the side. They didn't seem at all worried by our arrival although one or two could be heard to say "Eijin" (English people)—that is as opposed to Americans, and perhaps also the few Australians who had preceded us. Kiddies were shouting "Hello" or "Goodbye", words which they had inherited from the Americans, probably without really knowing what they meant. They were also waving us on frantically to the airfield, to whatever was awaiting us.

Feelings sink again

If our drive through Iwakuni's quaint little streets, and the mild but welcome greeting we had received, had calmed us down a little, there were alas still more shocks awaiting us, as we entered the station compound. We drove towards a very large and imposing building which was to be the BCAIR headquarters and which was, at least for the next six months or so, indeed to become my office and my home. The building had been the main building of the Japanese Naval Air Marine Corps referred to earlier. But, alas again, all was not what it seemed.

Chapter 4: Chain of Command

Our feelings sank. As soon as we entered the building we could see that everything inside was in complete disarray. It looked as if the whole place had been ransacked, possibly by the previous AMG occupants, just before they left, or possibly by local vandals, or by both. In half of the rooms there were no windows, doors, or ceilings. There was no central heating, hot water, or proper means of washing. We could not have been worse off in tents. Wash basins, mirrors, furniture, floor cloth, mats, electric light bulbs, were all mysteriously missing, though fittings and wall plugs etc. still remained as evidence that at one time they had been there. Rumour had it that scores of valuable first class Japanese parachutes had just been burned, rather than left for our use. The enthusiasm I had had at the beginning of my first day in Japan was wearing thin. For one day, it had been too much. I had really seen far too much. Sleep and a fresh day tomorrow were the only solution. But my purpose was thwarted again. My first night was almost sleepless. Our bedding had been left behind, and we had to improvise as well as we could. I found an odd radiator, and I huddled close to that (covered by a couple of old mackintoshes); but, by 11 pm, the temperature had cooled and I was left hugging a cold piece of metal.

Chapter 5

The Early days

Air Officer Administration (AOA)
A cock was crowing not far away. That was my signal for a fresh new day, and the start of my second day in Japan. There was nothing for it but to get up and stroll, but I didn't expect to derive much enjoyment from it. No one wanted to talk about yesterday. Like me, everyone was feeling a little glum at our prospects. Very early that morning, I was summoned to meet the most senior officer on the camp, the Air Officer Administration (AOA), while the future Commanding officer of BCAIR, Air Vice Marshal Bouchier, had still to arrive. The AOA was extremely re-assuring in our discussions but I was, inwardly at least, still very anxious.

"Have you ever done Organisation work before?"
"No Sir"
"Hm, well it doesn't really matter, I suppose. Common sense, my boy—that's all you want".

"There is a very big task waiting ahead for all of us. We have to build up and accommodate the first ever British Commonwealth Air Force—with forces from Australia, New Zealand, India, and the UK. All of them will be arriving, piecemeal unit by unit, over the next four months and, as I said when I visited you on board your ship in Bombay just before

Chapter 5: The Early days

you left for Japan, none of these personnel, during their stay in Japan, must ever have to *live under canvas*. If necessary, whatever is needed will have to be requisitioned from the local population.

"Much of this work", he continued, "will fall on the shoulders of Org. 3, which is your official title".

I was to harbour no illusions. There would be difficult problems to solve, and a lot of hard ground work to do, but common sense would see me through. At the moment I was the only BCAIR Staff officer here, but there was an Australian Squadron Leader here, who had been here in Iwakuni since January, and he, temporarily, would be my superior. On what we two did together much would depend, and how right these words proved to be. I was greatly cheered by hearing that I would not be alone. A few minutes later, the AOA introduced me to Squadron Leader Jock Ogilvie of the Royal Australian Air Force, whom I later always addressed simply as "Jock". I took to him immediately. For me he was a stroke of utmost good fortune. He became not only my mentor and friend, but also my saviour. His Scots accent, his pleasant lack of worry, and friendly attitude did so much during my first half hour with him to cement a permanent friendship. Initially at least, there were no intervening officers in the large gap between us and the AVM/AOA. As Org. 3, I would be reporting directly to them; and we had to keep both the AVM and the AOA fully aware of whatever was happening, both on the camp and off it, if it in any way related to BCAIR. At this stage of operations almost all incoming administrative correspondence to BCAIR came across my desk, although I never opened anything which was personally addressed. I didn't perhaps realise at the time the power and influence which this role gave me, but the future was suddenly bright again. I would be a poor man in such circumstances not to make the best use of my chance to learn all I could about Japan. In such a mood, my previous good humour revived. I was insensitive to the grey morning's biting cold. As I looked through the window at the distant mountains which were dressed in mist, I thought to myself the future is beckoning. The future is up to me. As to my title, Org. 3, I was perhaps too fond of it. I never wanted to change it, even when later it would have paid me handsomely to do so. This occurred for example when I was required to define the work of the

Organisation branch itself. Obviously the Org. 1 and Org. 2 slots would have more power, rank, and privilege than Org. 3, but for some reason I stuck stubbornly to Org. 3. Very mistakenly, I must have thought that Org. 3 would continue to have the same important influence on events as I had always had. AVM Bouchier himself also seemed to be as fond of the Org. 3 title as I was. At the end of my tour, completely on his own initiative, and to my absolute surprise, he very kindly wrote a very favourable letter of recommendation for me. He stressed how important Org. 3 had been in the build up of BCAIR, and that he had personally chosen me for the job. I still have his letter to this day.

Refurbishing BCAIR HQ

The first priority of our first few days in Iwakuni was to get our headquarters shipshape. Our best means of doing this was to employ mainly local labour. For purely domestic and administrative work, there was no shortage of female labour of all ages and talents of all sorts from clerks, typists, kitchen staff, cleaners, cooks, personal assistants, or whatever. I don't know how much they were paid for their work but it must have been adequate. For male labour, there was a different procedure in force, which at first caused me some personal disquiet, and with which I will deal with later under our daily routine. This was the so called daily muster of all men and youths between the ages of 16 and 60 who were virtually conscripted each day to do any required physical and manual work in and around the camp. To my relief, this was by no means as frightful as I had thought. On occasions, it was even good humoured and, from it, we found most of our very much needed carpenters, plumbers, painters, and decorators for the building's refurbishment. They were also paid, I believe; but, if so, it was probably very cheap labour, and one of the perks to which an Occupation Force was entitled. It also played a valuable part in getting our rooms habitable and our offices tidy and suitably furnished. Before my arrival several people had worked, lived, and slept in the great big central office upstairs, simply because it was the only warm room in the building. But since this room was very soon to become the AVM's office, we had no alternative but to evict the occupants. It had four large radiators, a linoleum covered floor, panelled walls, and a large oilcloth topped table. There was an officious air of serious business about the room, and I could already imagine the very many important

Chapter 5: The Early days

meetings which would eventually take place there. Many famous VIP's and other dignitaries from across the world were destined to cross its threshold. We were successful in restoring the building probably to its former glory. Many years later, the building was destroyed by fire and then rebuilt. I revisited it in 1990, when it had been returned again to US Army control. It was still a very impressive and imposing building. I was very kindly shown round the restored building by a United States Army major; and this evoked many fond memories of my days there. While we were refurbishing the building, we did as much as we could to make the place as suitable as possible, for living, working and relaxation; that is for accommodation, offices, the officers' Mess, catering, lounges, rest rooms, and even for dancing.

Accommodating HQ staff

Many HQ people, including myself, were accommodated in the main building. We allocated rooms to each other as fairly as we could. The rooms, when refurbished, were quite attractive with wash basins. I eventually shared a very pleasant room 69 on the ground floor with an Australian Wartime correspondent Jack Evans, who had an honorary rank of Flying Officer. Whereas previously, we officers would have had the help of a batman for personal matters, in Japan we were assigned young Japanese girls from the city. They were I suppose bat-women or maids, but we didn't use these terms. We just called them room girls. I was assigned Fusae San, a very pleasant 17 year old local girl (with whom I am still in contact after all these years). She kept our room clean, did general chores, and generally looked after us, our clothes, laundering, and so forth. As regards the building itself, a very pressing need was to get the hot water system working properly. There were elaborate boilers and washing areas with showers and baths in a very wide open area at the end of a long corridor on to which our room led. When all the rooms were again properly connected to the hot water system, it was once more a very efficient system. I can never remember it failing. I used to take showers there whenever I felt like it, and I soon got used to the many young female Japanese assistants who always seemed to be going through the area on some errand or other; but invariably they never paid the least bit of attention to us washing ourselves entirely in the nude. I soon lost any self consciousness which I may have had. When this work was completed, our living in Japan became very much more pleasant and interesting. We certainly couldn't complain since we were after all, receiving a generous hard living allowance! With the Exchange rate at the time also very high, at 960 Yen to a Pound, who would possibly dare to complain?

A home for the AVM

Very early on, just before Air Vice Marshal Bouchier was due to arrive, I went with our RAF Regiment officer, Flying Officer Bill Bolster, with whom I later also worked on requisitioning, to deliver furniture to a luxurious residence which was to become the AVM's future home in Iwakuni. Three other officers it was said would be living there but, if so, I never knew who they were, or if they ever did. Certainly, AVM Bouchier used to accommodate every important visitor there—and there were very many, who later came to see him. On this occasion, Bill Bolster and I were greeted, as I believe all visitors were, by three delightful young Japanese girls dressed in lovely kimonos with whom I tentatively tried out my Japanese. I was tremendously impressed by the AVM's residence. It was known as Kikkawa House and had been taken over from a Japanese Viscount Kikkawa, an elderly Japanese nobleman, whose wife was still living in a wing of the house. We didn't see her. The viscount had renounced his title in favour of his son; but, very soon after the end of the war, all Japanese nobility (Kizoku) disappeared and seem to have melted into normal society. A few days after our delivering his furniture, the AVM came to the office which we had previously prepared for him, and we gathered there to greet him. He gave us a very encouraging, patriotic, and inspiring speech about a great Commonwealth of which we should be proud. We were ambassadors to show the flag and what it stood for. It was a good inspiring talk which we all enjoyed.

Privileged guest of the AVM

A week or so later, possibly as a Thank You to Org. 3 for its help in furnishing the AVM's home, I was invited to have dinner with him. I was driven there in style in a limousine and was again greeted on my arrival in just the same way as before by the three pretty girls in their lovely kimonos. I have no actual notes of the occasion but as far as I can remember I was the only guest there that evening. Bill Bolster, who had done far more than me in getting the furniture in

Chapter 5: The Early days

place, was certainly not there. However, since the AVM later promoted Bill, by two jumps at one go to become a Squadron Leader for his expertise on the Parade ground, he was eventually amply rewarded. The AVM's faithful retainer, RAF Warrant Officer White, was discretely in attendance behind the AVM throughout the evening meal. What I most remember of the evening was my introduction to drinking sherry in a lovely bowl of hot tomato soup, which I enjoyed tremendously, but which I don't think I have ever since repeated. My recollection of the evening's conversation, apart from the AVM's interest in Org. 3, and my attitude towards it, seems to have been very general. I do have a vague memory of agreeing with the AVM wholeheartedly that two of the greatest Englishmen who have ever lived were William Shakespeare and Sir Winston Churchill. I was not surprised many years later to read in the AVM's biography, "Spitfires in Japan" that the AVM still strongly believed this. I was of course highly privileged to have been invited by the AVM to his residence that evening, since our two ranks were so wide apart (five huge steps). Whether this may be true or not, I had a strange feeling of protection there which stayed with me until the day I left Japan. It later showed itself to me in a variety of ways, which will become apparent as my tale continues.

Sad disposal of swords at sea

As soon as we had arrived at what was to be our HQ building on the 1st March, as I noted earlier, we had heard rumours that scores of valuable Japanese parachutes had been destroyed because no one knew what to do with them. We were reminded of this again a few days later when a room, which was momentarily kept locked, was found to contain even more valuable contents,—scores and scores of precious Japanese swords and scabbards. There were many weapons enthusiasts in our camp of course, who would dearly have loved to claim one of the swords and taken it home as a treasure of war. We could well imagine such treasures being shown off at home with pride. Could the claim for such a sword, however, ever be justified in this case, and on what basis? If ever we had decided to go down this route it would undoubtedly have led to a lot of bad feeling and bickering. Instead we reported the findings to both BCOF HQ and the American Military Government. Their reply was unequivocal. The swords and scabbards must be destroyed immediately, if possible by dumping them at sea.

Air Ministry, back in the UK, who somehow also seemed to have heard of our problem, echoed the same conclusion. When we pointed out to our own "high command", our AVM and the AOA, what a crying shame this would be, they were similarly equally determined. You have heard the decision. Do it! And so, on one lovely sunny morning in the ever beautiful Inland Sea, a group of us set off together with our doomed cargo in a smallish motor boat on our shameful mission. A little later, a few miles out to sea, so many lovely shining blades of silver glistening in the sunlight under a perfectly blue sky, were simply stacked on deck, and then scattered one at a time into the all too eagerly waiting waters below. They were no more; they had been dumped at sea as directed. What a tragic shame it seemed. And yet, perhaps after all, there was in the circumstances no other way of dealing with such a valued treasure. The liaison officer, called Hank, who had been sent to accompany us on the mission, who spoke with an American voice, and whom I had first met in Singapore on our way to Japan, had the same feelings as I did. I never did find out whether he was part of the UK liaison office in Tokyo or the American one. I did feel, however, that I could have made a very staunch friend of him. He stayed with us a few days more, and we had several photographs of us taken together. On our way back to Iwakuni and land, we soon forgot our sorrows. We all enjoyed to the full the wonderful boat trip back, savouring every minute of the beautiful seascape which was all around us.

Chapter 6

The Namiwaki's—A Glimpse of Family Life

Mrs Namiwaki, Shizue and her younger brother
From almost the very moment of my arrival in Japan, I had the very good fortune to meet and to socialise with Japanese families. The first of these wonderful families, some of which became lifelong relationships, was the Namiwaki family to whom I was introduced by Squadron Leader Jock Ogilvie, within days of arriving in Iwakuni. From the very second day of my stay in Japan, Jock had become not only a trusted guide and friend but, in all our activities, it was as if we shared a single mind. Our thoughts and our reaction to events were identical. The Namiwaki family, which Jock had already met many times, consisted of Mrs Namiwaki (a widow), her daughter Shizue who was aged about 19 or 20, and Shizue's younger brother Yukiyoshi, who was about three years his sister's junior. He was still at school. Mr. Namiwaki, the father of the family, was no longer alive but in his day he had been a very powerful business magnate in Tokyo. They were a rally delightful family. Together with Jock, I found that their home was such a pleasant relief from the early discomfort of our camp that we probably leaned on them far more than we should have. I derived not only some priceless information about conditions in Japan at the time, but I also enjoyed a lot of entertainment and happiness from

their kind and generous hospitality. In those early days there had been no mention of any forthcoming anti-fraternisation laws; and so, in no way did we ever feel inhibited in socialising with the family. Jock had come to know the Namiwaki's from their daughter, Shizue, who was employed as an interpreter at the airfield.

Shizue, a girl of hidden talent

Shizue was a, small, slightly plump, young lady who spoke perfect English, although, at least to me at that time, she had seemed rather timid and shy and rather too easily frightened into silence. This I felt would almost certainly put her at a disadvantage when interpreting for the Allied Forces. Many of the interpreters I had met in my early days in Japan had impressed me by their self confidence and sometimes their exuberance in showing off their skills. In fact, I sometimes felt (perhaps a little unfairly) that secretly they enjoyed letting us know that they could do for us, many things, like interpreting, which we were not capable of doing for ourselves. Fortunately, and most delightfully, when later, after a break of a few weeks, I met up with Shizue again, her manner and presence had changed beyond recognition. I had never seen a character so wonderfully transformed in such a short time. She had become so much more self confident, dynamic, and indeed impressive. Her talents had obviously been hidden from view. I will refer to this remarkable transformation, in some very different circumstances, much later in my story, by which time she had been appointed to a different post serving the Occupation Forces. She had also become a prominent committee member of the local Iwakuni Cultural Society. Indeed, at this second time around in my personal experience, she became a personal treasure to me, helping me to make some speeches to the Society. Within two to three months or so, she had become such a changed person; so transformed, that I found it hard to believe. It was certainly gratifying to know that, someone like Shizue, who really had talent, could still (despite some initial troubles) come shining through to such very good effect, for the benefit of us all. Perhaps the social interaction, and the experience of conversing with Jock and me, had helped in some small way to give her the confidence she eventually acquired. It would be good to think that we had, after all, given her something in return for her family's kindness to us.

Chapter 6: The Namiwaki's—A Glimpse of Family Life

Visits and trips along the river

Returning, however, to my early days with the family, Jock and I spent many pleasant afternoons in the company of the family. Our visits were mainly at weekends when we could get away from our ever increasing workload at the office. We might spend a pleasant afternoon taking tea at their home, or we might rent a boat and take a pleasant little trip upstream with Shizue and Yukiyoshi, and then sit beside a gently, flowing river, beneath some rocky pine clad mountain pathways, drinking tea, munching a few biscuits, and throwing pebbles into the water. In Japanese, we would count the resulting ripples on the surface of the water, and I would try to talk as much in Japanese as I could but without leaving Jock out of the conversation, although his Japanese was rapidly improving. Back at their home, while an evening meal was being prepared, we would listen to music, Brahms, Wagner, and various western classics, German ballads, English folksongs,— as well as Japanese compositions. We would talk about our families and their aims and hopes in life. It was very interesting to listen to Yukiyoshi and to hear directly the views of a Japanese teenager. He was a very bright youngster, and much less shy than his sister in wanting to talk about their future. He was preparing for his Middle School examinations; he was very keen to practise his English; and he was concerned that the examination would require a fair knowledge of England and its geography—subjects which inevitably in Japan had been neglected during the war. I was very pleased to learn just before I left Japan, at the end of September, that he had passed his examination with flying colours. Our discussions would continue over the evening meal. Indeed, it was the Namiwaki family with whom I had my first meal in a Japanese home. I enjoyed selecting from the myriad of little dishes put before me, and even the so called raw fish (sashimi) had an immediate attraction for me. But I regretted very much that t was not at all skilful in using my hashi (chopsticks). It was a wonderful introduction into Japanese home life and a gloriously new experience for me.

Chapter 7

Daily Routine at the Camp

Title: Org. 3

As time rolled by we became much more organised. As Org. 3, I was in charge with Jock, directly under the AOA, of all administrative and domestic matters; and, in the very early days especially, I reported personally even to Air Vice Marshal Bouchier. Jock and I helped to get the headquarters properly equipped, and its staff accommodated. Our responsibility for this work continued but that initial job was now largely done. Almost all incoming mail and documents addressed to HQ BCAIR still came across my desk however. Jock and I were responsible for any activities which involved the local populace, including the very unpleasant business of requisitioning peoples' property and possessions. We had to keep aware of all visitors to our area from other parts of Japan; visitors, for example, like local Education and Liaison officers, and even visitors from the Commonwealth and the United States. If our AOA or AVM hadn't previously been advised of a visit, it was our duty to let them know well in advance who was likely to be arriving. Org. 3 was even asked if we had any objections to the arrival of our own Service people and officials, should they be arriving independently of our main forces or units. I remember quite distinctly for example a signal coming across my desk about the

Chapter 7: Daily Routine at the Camp

arrival of a certain Flt Lt. Cortazzi, and another fellow officer, fairly early in my tour. Flt Lt. Cortazzi became a very distinguished author of books and articles on Japan and did a great deal to foster good Anglo-Japanese relations. He was British Ambassador to Japan from 1980 to 1984, and Chairman of the Japan Society in the UK 1985-95. Somewhat surprisingly, I never met Flt Lt. Cortazzi, while he was in Japan, although he was at that time a member of the Provost and Security Section in Iwakuni City. However, by some strange quirk of fate, he did later meet up with Shizue Namiwaki to whom I referred in the previous chapter. She worked in his section as an interpreter/translator, and apparently kept in touch with him for many years after that. Among our other duties, Org 3 was responsible for interpreting, and passing on to our troops, what we understood was official AMG and BCOF policy. Occasionally, instructions and guidance also came directly from the Air Ministry in the UK, the British Council in London, and from Commonwealth countries. Directives also came down to us from General MacArthur's HQ in Tokyo. Org. 3's "office" was a large, very pleasant room, at the front of the building on the first floor. There was plenty of space around me waiting for fellow occupants to arrive later. My desk had a splendid glass top for its entire surface and was adjacent to, and next to, a door leading directly into the office of the Air Officer Admin (AOA). I was also only one door away from Air Vice Marshal Bouchier. There wasn't a job too big, too small, or too menial, to be handled by Jock or by me. Telephone calls came from Kure, from our two out airfields in Bofu and Miho, from Tokyo, and from anywhere at all. They never ceased. Reams of instructions and documents arrived daily. It was a long time afterwards before anyone wanted to speak to anyone else but Org. 3. Jock and I were an "Information Bureau". We had the facts and we "knew everything" that was going on. Even when other staff officers arrived and began to take over some of the work, we tended to hold on to as many jobs as we could. Despite all this, we still found many ways to enjoy exploring Japan. It was, however, never at the expense of my work. I often returned to my room in the evenings between tea and dinner and lay on the bed exhausted, mentally and physically, as I had done in the heat of India. Here, however, there was no heat to blame for the problem. It was due entirely to pressure of work. If, later, I suppose I may technically have broken some rules on fraternisation, no other officer could have been more loyal and hard working than I was.

Piecemeal build up of our forces

Neither the AOA, nor anyone, had really explained to me the implications of a piecemeal, unit by unit, build up of our forces. Perhaps I should have worked out the nature of the problem myself. I was even not sure that anyone "back home" had thought about it. Politically,— did anyone really care? Post war Britain had enough problems on its hands without having to organise an Occupation Force at the other side of the world. The situation for us, who had just arrived, however, was very different. The piecemeal build up of forces, little by little, was very real, very near to us, and very trying. There was no basic infra structure on which we could depend, even sometimes for our most basic needs. Right up to the time we arrived in Kure, our voyage and everything connected with it, had been managed for us beautifully by British and Indian forces, which were well practised in moving people across the globe. We had no worries; all our needs were well taken care of. We could well have been on a holiday cruise. After Kure, however, the situation for us was completely different. Two months previously, the United States Army had vacated what was now the BCOF area of Japan and had handed over responsibility for it to the Australians. The unit of the United States Army, which had been there until then, had been a self contained and well equipped force, well able to look after itself. In contrast, very little of BCOF or BCAIR, was ever assembled in advance. We were not self contained and, unlike the American army, we were being built up abroad, little by little. At first we had few personnel and very few resources. When I arrived in Iwakuni on the 1st of March 1946, the Australians, during their first two months in BCOF, had built up some resources of food, medicine, money, and transport etc. in both Kure and Iwakuni; and, we were very grateful to be able to depend on them, whenever we could, for their very welcome services. There was no BCAIR as such, and certainly no BCAIR HQ. Then, suddenly, as from 1st March, we had a BCAIR with a headquarters which was little more than a model—trying gradually to become operational. Personnel like me, who had joined the HQ well ahead of others, had the job not only of preparing for, accommodating, and building up BCAIR forces as the AOA had said, but we also had the job of looking after ourselves. We

Chapter 7: Daily Routine at the Camp

had no blue print or detailed instructions to follow except the one, to which I referred earlier, which was to ensure that none of our personnel should ever have to live under canvas.

The daily muster of manual labour

All Japanese men and youths aged between 16 and 65 (including doctors, clerks, shop keepers, dentists, technicians, butchers, bakers, and all manner of labourers, both skilled and unskilled), were required to assemble daily behind our headquarters building. The workers were then forcibly employed on any and every kind of work which needed to be done. Fortunately, the muster turned out not to be so distasteful or brutal as it sounded (and, as I had feared). It is hard to describe such a varied mixture of people as those who paraded at the camp for us each morning. As we looked out from our offices, we could see there were some workers who looked like sun browned diggers, and some who even looked like convicts, dressed in flimsy loin cloths who, completely unmindful of their attire, would parade with pick axes, spades, and hammers, and ceaselessly toil each day on some selected piece of hard unyielding ground. Among them, there was also always the swarthy tubby plumber, wearing a dusty brown fawn hat with a turned down brim, whose services were forever in constant demand. There were men who looked industrious, but who were not skilled, and there were men who argued, but they were not really bad humoured. There were ill clad labourers, who were not labourers by trade; but ordinary local people who had just been conscripted for a daily job. They were often required to carry heavy desks, chairs and cupboards, from one part of the building to another. They must have wondered "whatever for?", and must have believed that we in the HQ were just quite mad. These enforced workers, who were tremendously useful to us in many ways, came to us regularly each morning in open trucks. Whether at work or taking a rest, they could invariably be seen carrying their venerable bento, or food boxes, for lunch. Under the eagle eyes of their foremen and controllers they were obviously not as natural and artless as they would be in their freer moments. They were often harried and frustrated. However, we did find that they were not at all ill disposed to a chat or a "special request". With favours asked for by our troops on the one hand, and chiding by their supervisor for wasting time on the other, the workers were at a loss to know what to do. Some officers and I no less, were the principal offenders. We would seize on an electrician to fix a lamp to a table, or a light for our beds, or we would call a carpenter to repair some furniture, which we could have gone without, but never once, although they had the right to refuse, did we ever find an unwilling hand. All those we asked were eager to do our little jobs and, whilst doing them, engage in conversation with us. The foreman had to try almost the impossible,—to be popular both with his team, and with us. It was all part of a familiar everyday picture.

Requisitioning

Undoubtedly, the most unpleasant task, which the Occupation Force had to do, was requisitioning; literally the taking away, of property and possessions of the local population in order to accommodate our troops. As part of a Peace agreement, a defeated country undertakes with the victors to make reparations, to maintain the victor's Occupation Force at a specified strength, and to meet the force's permanent needs. A defeated country may therefore be called on to meet all the Occupation Forces' accommodation requirements, in other words to provide and furnish its barracks, rest rooms, offices, Messes, and to provide the necessary labour to do this. A target for requisitioning could be any standing building (public or private), a library, factory, firm, store room, council building, or whatever. Compensation might be paid, but this was trifling, and often there was no appeal. That it could be done at all, while at the same time maintaining good relations with the dispossessed people is almost unbelievable. It is certainly a tribute to those who managed to do it, that we did it amicably, as we did in many cases. That it was done so well was due to the early work of Australian Squadron leader, Jock Ogilvie, from whose guidance I had learned and gained so much. He had arrived in Iwakuni in early January 1946, seemingly alone, with almost unlimited powers to survey the scene and find out as much as he could of its structure; how it functioned, and how we as an occupying force should relate to it. In doing what he did, and how he did it, he earned the total respect of every inhabitant in Iwakuni. No one challenged his word. He was liked by all and he had no enemies, despite some harrowing cases which from time to time emerged. In all his many dealings, Jock's unique understanding of the relationship between victor and vanquished, and his guidance and common sense approach to problems, pervaded everything we did. Jock believed (and I always tried to emulate him closely) that the attitude of the procurer was often more important to the local Japanese people than the value of all the things which were ultimately requisitioned. No one can be expected to give up their personal property gladly, but he showed that it may at least be done humanely and more willingly, if the procurers go about their business kindly, quietly, and with tact. Initially, Jock and I attended, or were nominally in charge of all requisitions; but eventually other people followed us. Later on, restrictions on procurement were also applied by the American Military Government, exempting certain articles from procurement, but I often felt that requisitioning was much abused. I also very much regretted the attitude and sometimes uncharitable expressions of a few would-be procurers, which hopefully were never heard; or, at least, if they were heard, they were never understood by the Japanese people who were there.

Harrowing experiences

The problem of finding barrack rooms for our troops was eased sometimes, because of the custom of certain firms and factories in the Iwakuni area to provide their workers with living accommodation on site. In some cases, dormitories and living quarters, which could easily be converted into barracks, already existed. We still had the job of meeting factory owners, tenants, and other representatives, and then getting them to comply with our plans. It was a painful process, but by taking say only half of a factory, which was probably doing only half of its normal work anyhow; and, by making other compromises, we did eventually find solutions. But lots of people were still being evicted and losing their work places, and not only that, some were being robbed of their only home. I wondered what my parents would have felt, if they had had half of their business taken away from them. Or, how anyone would feel to be in possession of something taken from those who had previously owned it, and for whom it may have been extremely precious. But, I was nothing but an involuntary tool in the system. I was helpless, so far as the law was concerned, and unable to make much of a difference. There were even more disturbing occasions. "Why do you want all this room?" shouted one indignant soul, to a would-be procurer, who wanted to take over a building which was being used for aged and homeless people. It was a remark which was made all the more pathetic by the dilapidated and tumbledown condition in which we found the place. It would never have been of use to us anyhow. Yet, the would-be procurer was prepared to take it, and to let it remain out of use until he could think of a purpose for it. "But, you can't take it" cried a whimpering and pathetic little man. I felt nauseated. But how right the occupant was! On an appeal, the American Military Government finally said "No". It was our first defeat, and I could not have been more pleased. Common sense and fair play had finally triumphed. I dropped out of much of the direct "requisitioning" work, after a month or so; but Jock carried on; and others followed when he left. For me, they were always very harrowing experiences. It was never a duty one could do with enthusiasm.

Chapter 8

Appreciation From Girls at the Camp

Invaluable support for Allied troops

It is remarkable, and it was a great blessing of good fortune for us at the camp, especially in the early days, when everything was so strange, that we were so well supported and sustained by the Japanese girls we employed there. Their very presence cheered the atmosphere. Their devotion and loyalty to us, and the work which they did for us, was invaluable beyond words. I don't imagine for a minute that many of the girls had ever intended to embark on domestic careers and much less to work for troops who had occupied their country. However, the war had brought about many changes; and the girls were enjoying the innovation. They now possessed a little "ko-gane" or pocket money, and they were no doubt also attracted by the food which we offered to those who worked for us, and which was valued out of all proportion to its pre-war worth. It was our practice to give food to employees at the camp, firstly because we always had food left over and it would have been a crime to waste it; and, secondly, because it persuaded the girls to do work for us which they might otherwise have declined. The work, however, was for long hours, from early morning until late at night. The girls were also dealing with foreigners about whom they knew very little; except, that is, what their propaganda ministry had told them. At first, by accident or otherwise, it seemed that some girls of doubtful reputation may have been engaged, but they had soon been dismissed as evidence came to light. It is not to be wondered at, that many girls may have suffered slander and insults at the hands of some of their compatriots, who labelled them collaborationists or worse. Such cat calling was not always in the open, of course, for fear that our Intelligence security might take note and retaliate; but, I did occasionally hear of, and see, instances of its existence. Such events served only to strengthen our appreciation and admiration for the girls who were working for us. Their devotion and simple charm was unsurpassable. With one nod of their heads, a flick of their eyes, or a twitch of the mouth, we were flattered. Charm, natural grace, modesty, artless beauty, gentility, and tenderness,—it was hard to resist. It was understandable that we should become attached to them. No tribute to them was ever too high. "Not for a hundred thousand years" wrote Lafcadio Hearn, to whom I referred in Chapter 1, "will such a type of woman appear again."

A special show for a departing Squadron

A good example of such devotion and sentiment arose, when the Australian Fighter Squadron and its HQ, which had been based in the camp with us, was transferred to Bofu, a camp some forty miles away on the west coast of Japan. A number of room girls, waitresses, and girls doing work in the Officers' Mess, had asked us imploringly from the "depths of their hearts" to do a few "stage turns" which, they said, would be a token of their good will towards the Australian officers who were leaving. The girls' friendly wish, as a mark of their appreciation was to sing and dance for us, and to give us a flavour of real Japan. Going back stage in my official capacity, I was struck by the infinite beauty, prettiness, and excitement of all the gaily dressed girls. It was at this point that I first met Emiko Miyazaki, who was outstanding, but I didn't know then how much more friendly we were destined to become. All the girls were truly wonderful and tireless. Their bright and cheerful kimonos, on that dull late afternoon, gladdened my heart. Each single kimono, I soon learned, told a different story. In no other country in the world does dress betray the age of the wearer so sharply. I felt that I was, literally, able to judge the ages of people from the kimonos they wore. The more gaily coloured the kimono, the younger was the

Chapter 8: Appreciation From Girls at the Camp

wearer. The custom it seemed was rigidly observed on this occasion. I had not seen such bright and cheerful colours for a long time. My travels through Kure and Hiroshima, and my sojourn in Iwakuni until now, had been tinged with dark shades of sadness, framed as it were in black. The clothes which the girls wore at work too were often dull and uninteresting. Many girls wore Western sweaters and Japanese women's' trousers. I was beginning to lose my sense of colour. But here at last, there was life and energy. Japan had been hiding itself from us for all this time. Now, as a measure of their appreciation for Australian kindness as they saw it, the girls were removing their veil. What appealed to us most was their complete lack of falsity, sophistication, and sham. Some were very good looking, some were plainer. Some had small cute figures, and some were homely and more ordinary, but that didn't matter at all. The scene merged into a perfect whole,—beautifully adorable,—adorably beautiful. No one could have wished for more.

Message from the show and our response

The girls' message to us was clear and obviously heartfelt, and our response was ecstatic. We could not have felt more gratitude. I was asked to translate the song and dance titles, and the little opening and closing speeches. "This evening, we would like to give you a little exhibition of Japanese song and dance, and while doing so, engrave in our own hearts our memories of your beautiful spirit and so rebuild a true, faithful, and peaceful Japan . . . . we bid you all Good health, Good luck, and Farewell . . . and so on. I was also expected to interpret quickly and accurately many almost incoherently excited words of thanks from the audience. I remember one officer who was quite perturbed at my translating into Japanese, in a few short words, something which had taken him about half a dozen sentences to utter in English. I was by no means a professional interpreter. Some of the dances they did for us were tales of valour of a previous era, of youth in bloom, of love affairs between a lord and his maid, of romantic drama, and of one called "the tale of a dismal journey, and tragedy". We had no magical stage effects to draw on to help them, and the girls were possessed of nothing else but their lovely kimonos and their fans or sensu, which at times in our imagination became swords, umbrellas, walking sticks, flutes, and all other kinds of disparate devices in turn.

- 45 -

This was a highlight of my earliest days in Japan. I often spoke about it afterwards to Emiko Miyazaki, but she would never accept any praise for her performance. I sometimes doubted if she remembered that it had been I who had done the interpreting that evening, because it was several weeks after wards before we really met. I often saw her around the camp of course. She would have been difficult to escape one's eye; but, except for knowing that she worked for Jock, I knew very little about her. At the end of the show, we invited all our splendid actresses to appear on the stage. I stood there with Mama San or the elder girl, who was presumably their producer, to thank them for their marvellous performance. We stood there between a blaze of colour from the girl's lovely kimonos on the one hand, and a sea of royal deep blue Australian Air Force uniforms, on the other. The audience had been entertained beyond its dreams. The Australians present were absolutely overwhelmed and over joyous. The English officers there perhaps were a little more reserved, reflecting their national characteristics, but there was no doubt that everyone had been treated to a really most delightful occasion. I was later privileged to hear more such enjoyable Japanese music, and also to see lots of dancing, in the months ahead, but I never really captured again these first impressions of seeing it for the first time performed by some young pretty girls dancing for the sheer love of it; and, with such perfectly co-ordinated movement of hand, foot, and body. Many weeks later, when the fraternisation laws began to arrive on my desk (to which I will be referring later), I thought how lucky we had been to have seen such a wonderful show at all. Such open friendship, especially at the camp itself under its new anti-fraternisation regime, would have been strictly taboo. But, in fact, if it were really known, this was nevertheless just the kind of personal interaction, which was needed to help us do our work; and, it is why—though I say it myself—we were so successful. This is true, whether we were painfully requisitioning property; or, hopefully, helping Japan to find its way back to democracy, and to becoming again a self respecting nation.

Chapter 9

Party-Going and the Story of a Geisha

Fukugawa Ryokan

The Fukugawa ryokan was a very convenient and splendid, Japanese, family run, hotel, just a couple of streets back from the river front. Here, too, was the famous Iwakuni Golden Bridge (Kintai bashi) with its five beautiful spans,—at high tide, stretching picturesquely across a lovely fast flowing Nishiki river. We sometimes met town officials there, or we retreated there after meetings at work. In the early days before anti-fraternisation, the Fukugawa ryokan was also a very pleasant environment in which to relax with some of the young girls from the camp,—particularly with the interpreters and girls from the typing pool;—especially, on a Saturday evening, after a very busy and tiring week. I joined the parties which were held there, and indeed I often took an active part in organising them. When I revisited the Fukugawa in 1990, during a holiday, which I spent in Japan, that is 44 years later, Mrs Fukugawa still recognised me. She introduced me to her son who probably had not been born when I was there before. But now, he was part owner and director of the huge magnificent, international hotel (the Iwakuni Kokusai Kanko hotel) on the river front, just at the foot of the Kintai bashi. I had lunch at the Kokusai Kanko hotel with Mrs Fukazawa's son, and he invited me to stay the night there too. But, I had only one night left in Iwakuni at the time, so I said I would prefer to stay at the ryokan, if only to remind me of my very happy times there. I had not of course ever spent a night there before. Back in early 1946, I had attended several little parties there which had been very successful and very pleasant, with plenty of music and dancing. But, then, for some reason, the parties suddenly ceased. A little time later, I heard that a party was being held to which I had not been invited. Flying Officer Bolster, the RAF Regiment officer, whom I mentioned earlier, was one of the organisers; and, although for some reason, which became clearer later, he seemed reluctant to invite me, he did finally relent; and I went along. Tragically it turned out (as I will recall in the next section) to be something very different from what I had expected. It was not one of our very likeable, little Saturday evening, parties. I sincerely wished, afterwards, that it hadn't happened, and that I hadn't been there. My great friend and mentor, Squadron Leader Jock Ogilvie, had no interest at all in party going; he always preferred more intimate person to person friendships. Hence, as far I can remember, I never discussed it, or its outcome, with him.

Different atmosphere/different participants

As soon as I entered the familiar guest room, where on previous occasions we had had so much fun, I realised that this was an entirely different situation. There were quite a few officers there, who were senior to me; and, as far as I could see, none of our young girls were there from BCAIR HQ. The womenfolk there were generally several years older than our camp girls, and hence were dressed in more sombre kimonos. I should perhaps have turned and run, but that might have seemed disrespectful; and, without my own transport, it would have been difficult. I had an inkling of what was to come; but, I decided to stick it out and to return to camp afterwards, in the transport which had been provided, in the normal way. I was not entirely naïve. I knew about the role of call girls, escorts, and others in society, who engaged in extra marital sexual activities, and especially the attraction which this type of activity had for troops who were serving away from home for long periods of time. We were frequently reminded of these dangers in talks by Air Vice Marshal Bouchier, our Commanding officer. He usually broached the subject extremely cleverly in his excellent "Show the Flag" talks, which I always liked to listen to. In Japan, of course, we

Chapter 9: Party-Going and the Story of A Geisha

had heard many tales about geisha which had heightened our interest. A genuine geisha girl was accomplished, intelligent, and talented, both in music and drama, having undergone several years of severe and rigorous training. The employment of geisha in Japan may not always have separated the moral from the immoral, but it seems to have been an acceptable part of Japanese society throughout the ages. It certainly separated the cultured from the crude. But, be all that as it may, I would still not have wanted to discuss the subject with either of the two lovely Japanese families, the Namiwaki's, or the Miyazaki's, the latter with whom I later became so closely acquainted.

Formal introductions

We went through the usual introductions and niceties found at any gathering, a little music, laughter, and drinks; and then the obvious intention of the evening which, in this case, was to divide (I imagined) into about a dozen pairs of people who would then discretely disappear without further word to anyone. I was left with a lady whom I will call Miss P. I didn't make a note of her name which now escapes me, although I do remember asking what it was. The next thing, I remember, I was with her in a small room, protesting that I had no intention of proceeding any further. My refusal to participate was greeted by absolute surprise and scorn, which she spluttered out from her mouth almost as if it was from a machine gun. At first, as she violently tossed her head backwards, I thought that the poor girl was hysterical; but, gradually she calmed down, muttering something about strange and fortunate wives,—one of whom she no doubt thought I had left at home, way back in my own country. She put away the quilt and clothes for the bed, which she had been arranging; and, suddenly, seemed eager to talk. I forgot all about the other guests who had wandered elsewhere, and who were no doubt now doing what had been their intention from the beginning. My conscience however was clear. I called for some tea for both of us, and I just listened. I said nothing.

Doomed from childhood

Miss P. told me a pitiful tale about how she had been removed from home life, at quite a tender age, and had literally been "sold into a geisha school in order to relieve the strain on her family's finances.

– 49 –

Several years before it happened, she had been made aware by her parents of the fate which awaited her, but this didn't lessen the shock when the day of her departure finally came. Her departure meant a permanent good bye to her relatives, friends, and surroundings; and, a headlong rush into the unknown. However, she had braced herself for her ordeal and had accepted her lot. She would be trained to sing, dance, and play, to speak correctly, to bear herself with educated grace and courtesy, and in short to be not a common call girl, but an elegant geisha?. There might, she hoped, be no dishonour, and no sordid life or harsh living conditions. There might even be a husband who would be kind, wealthy, and handsome, who would release her from her bondage. Such a happy fate was known to have happened in the past; and it could happen again. In any case there was nothing to be gained by brooding and regretting. She had had no alternative but to make the best of it; and that, she claimed, she had done. I was in no doubt that she had.

True stories and myths

I had heard many stories about the role of geisha in Japan, some of them perhaps true and some of them which were obviously exaggerated, or entirely false. Miss P.'s story was certainly not a myth. She was now hardened to life's hard knocks, and was well experienced in the part she had been destined to play. She had suffered the rigours of early discipline, and the disappointment of not becoming a member of a "refined society"; but she had emerged, as she said, as the mistress of her own art and charm, and a talented member of her profession. She was, of course, a very different person from the innocent waif surrendered by her father, eight or ten years earlier. She was probably more deserving of pity then, than now; but, as she had reminisced, so frankly with her tale, I could not help but feel a tinge of sympathy for her. Circumstances make us all what we are and what we become. For some, there are hardships, temptations, and trials in life. For others, it often seems, they have ease, contentment, and an ability to escape from danger. Miss P. might once even have escaped, she said, when a young widower of considerable means had signified his intentions of marrying her. This would have released her from the grips of her employers. It had, at the time, raised again the wildest fancies of her youth. I listened intently to every word she said but, except for a few

Chapter 9: Party-Going and the Story of A Geisha

polite interjection like, Oh dear, how sad, what a dreadful shame, and so on, I remained completely silent.

The impact of War

Unfortunately, the war had arrived and robbed Miss P. of her young widower who might have become her husband. This was as near as Miss P. ever came to good fortune; and it was, she said, an ironic twist in her fate. Her life during the war had fitted in with the chaos of the times. She had become a "comfort girl". With the occupation of Japan by Allied troops, she had regained freedom from her employers and her bondage to them. The Allies may have set her free by their actions; but, they had also brought temptation. For the geisha world, she said, the Occupation was a life saver, a renewal of hope, and a chance of prosperity. She was obviously not about to abandon this fruitful opportunity. She knew that she had charms and talents which were in demand. She was tied to her calling, just as much as any clerk to his counter, or any builder to his bricks? She had not expected me to answer. I was glad. It was not until she approached the present, when perhaps mistaking my silence for approval, and my interest for sympathy, that I felt a need to call a halt to her story, sad as it was. I may have appeared ungracious in ending her frank confessions rather abruptly, but that was certainly not my intention. I was in fact very appreciative of her frank and open story, and the self effacement which she had shown in telling it. I believed it was very much to her credit. For this reason alone, I had no hesitation in agreeing to her farewell request, not to mention the outcome of our meeting that evening to anyone. I realised that, if I were to do so, her reputation in the quarters which most mattered to her would have been seriously harmed. No action of mine, I resolved, should be the cause of that. I had no trouble in keeping my word. I told no one.

Mea culpa:

If I had thought that this was the end of my evening's experience and that I could then go back to camp and in my own quiet solitude, reflect on the evening's amazing events, I was sadly mistaken. I boarded the bus which had brought us to the Fukugawa ryokan; and, while I was waiting for others to join me, a group of Military Police swooped down on us, and wrote down our names, rank and unit. Those who were still in the Fukugawa ryokan were quizzed about what they had been doing there. I have no idea what they said. When the police had left, we were driven back to the camp as originally arranged, wondering whatever was going to happen to us. I spent quite an uncomfortable Sunday, wondering whatever could have possessed me to attend such a dubious party. The first thing I did on the following Monday morning was to visit a senior officer, a Wing Commander whom I knew in the Provost branch near the Headquarters, and I related to him the whole sorry story. Fortunately for us, the full force of the anti fraternisation laws was not yet in place. Had it been, the outcome may have been very different. My friendly Wing Commander said that since we had not been seen with Japanese girls in a moving vehicle (the really significant words seemed to be, the moving vehicle) he didn't believe we had committed any offence. At least, I heard no more about it. I dread to think what might have happened if it had been a few months later. The consequences didn't bear thinking about. Not for the first time, during my stay in Japan, it seemed that I had a protective angel looking after me!

Chapter 10

Happy Days with the Namiwaki's

Nothing is forever

Throughout all the above period, both Jock and I continued to spend some very happy times with the Namiwaki's. They satisfied completely our main social interest in Japanese family life. For both of us, a visit to the Namiwaki's was a very welcome relief, from some of our most harrowing duties. But, perhaps unwisely, we took our good fortune for granted; because, very unexpectedly and suddenly, there was a bombshell. Shizue had lost her job. Her position at the camp, as our principal camp interpreter, had been terminated. Some people said that Shizue had recently become incapable of interpreting, literally "word for word", the frequent angry exchanges between ill tempered Commonwealth officers' on the one hand, and possibly sometimes stubbornly complacent Japanese executives, on the other. Or, alternatively perhaps, Shizue was simply unwilling to be precisely literal; because she was too sensitive to the participants' feelings, and always far too eager to maintain friendly relations. To interpret too literally was, she deemed, rude and ill considered. Whatever the cause may have been, however, Shizue still remained Jock's favourite; and, certainly, if he had intervened, he had enough influence to retain her. But if he had done so, he knew that her position with the other girls would have become intolerable. I knew that Shizue had already been the subject of sarcasm from some girls, and that she had not stood up for herself as she could have done, so very easily. In order to continue to help Jock, and to keep in touch with him, she had showed her good character by offering to work in the kitchen; but, with kitchen work now far more foreign to her than her knowledge of English, she found herself in a worse plight. For kitchen usage, she probably didn't know the difference between the purpose of a basin and a bowl. She was, in short, a misfit. Instead of sarcasm and unkind glances from language rivals in the office, she was now also the target of cold hearted kitchen staff. Feeling humiliated, she ran away, seemingly broken in heart and spirit. She returned to her books and, under the wing of her mother, she settled down again to the kind of life of reading and study to which she was accustomed. I didn't know it then, of course, as I hinted earlier, that fate had destined that, within a month or so, I would meet up again with Shizue, in very different circumstances. For the moment, however, it seemed that the Namiwaki's may have walked out of our lives, forever. Our chances of meeting them again seemed very bleak indeed,

An unexpected Sunday visit

Then, shortly after the bombshell which we had suffered, Jock had contacted the Namiwaki's again, to pass on to them the remains of Shizue's salary. I had thought that the Namiwaki's might have taken this intrusion rather badly. However, as Jock explained to me later,— that, although the family might have all the money in the world, this would now be frozen; and, with father deceased, the amount of unearned income the family could now draw might be as low as 500 Yen per month, which was really a very paltry sum. The rice ration for this amount of money was only two thirds of the amount needed to survive. The remainder had to be bought in the Yamisoba or in the dark market. Jock also believed that it was most important that Shizue should find work. At last a letter did come from Shizue. She was obviously very fond of Jock, and looked upon him as a substitute for her father. I would have been surprised if she had not replied. Jock did have a fatherly disposition towards her, and we were overjoyed to learn that she was working again at the Met weather station attached to the City council. Jock's decision was to go in person, and he invited me to go with him, the following Sunday afternoon. We arranged a trip out to sea, and it turned out to be one of our most memorable afternoons and evenings we had ever spent with the family.

The Inland Sea at its best

It was the first Sunday I had been out without a coat and I was already regretting that I had followed Jock's advice to leave it behind. However, in brilliant sunshine, and beneath a perfectly blue sky, four of us, Jock, Shizue, Yukiyoshi, and I, boarded our rented little time worn launch. Two Japanese crewmen were standing by, wreathed in smiles, as we did so. Shizue and her brother were dressed almost in summer clothes, she in a loose fitting dress with a belt round her middle, and Yukiyoshi in flannels and white shirt. Both of them wore straw brimmers on their heads. They must have felt colder than I did. But it was lovely and fresh and we soon forgot the cold. We all felt full of life and exhilarated, in our little boat in the Inland Sea. We sped around, in and out and between the many little islands with their rugged time worn coast lines. We made for a lighthouse six miles out to sea—a pearl of the purest white—like an ivory castle rising out of a silver sea, its battlements tinged with gold by a gradually sinking sun. We then turned and raced at last towards some other boats whose" white sails in the sunset" were also reddening as they reflected the afternoon sky. It was heaven.

A splendid catch of fish

We pulled alongside and boarded some sailing boats, like pirates on the high seas, carrying off half their catch of fish which had just been hauled in with their nets. This included many odd looking fish the like of which I had never before seen. We paid of course for what we took. We would have stayed longer and watched their remaining nets being hauled aboard, but we had been tipped off that our Commanding officer, or his AOA, was also not very far away fishing in the area in his private launch. An encounter with him in the circumstances was not something we welcomed. Although Jock wouldn't admit it, I think he was as scared as I was of renewing our acquaintance with our two commanding officers in the company of our present companions. We returned, with fish and all, in our jeep to the Namiwaki's household. We wished to present them with the fish we had bought. It was a token of thanks, in part at least, for all the kindness they had shown us during the previous few weeks. Of course, they wouldn't dream of letting us go without partaking of some of the fish we had brought back with us; and so we were virtually forced to stay for yet another wonderful evening.

The Namiwaki's at home

Supper was soon being prepared and Jock was busy helping Shizue and her mother to grate the fish. It was so hard I couldn't believe it had ever been fish at all. When we all sat down together we were all facing a lovely looking meal. With the fish we had a few vegetables, steamed rice, rice balls, and lots of other goodies. It was an unforgettable little feast, followed by kaki or persimmon and green tea. I remember also my introduction to takeko or little bamboo shoots. Jock said he thought they tasted like wood, and were hard to eat, but I found them delicious and their toughness a pleasant contrast to the fish and other light delicacies which we had. The evening wore on just as beautifully. The table was cleared. We stretched our legs in relief from the squatting position, drank our tea, and chatted. In deference to Jock; but, more truthfully because it was easier, I gave up trying to speak in Japanese and spoke from then on in English. Mrs Namiwaki was encouraged and excited to show us her achievements in ikebana—an art in arranging flowers which has been famous in Japan from time immemorial. Photographs, books, and articles she had written or figured in were joyously revealed and explanations greatly appreciated both for the information behind the art and the sheer beauty of it. It was a wonder to see the big improvement that could be made in an arrangement merely by moving a few flowers and their leaves. When I compared this well considered care with what we so often see at home in England—where people are often content to take just a few seconds merely sticking a bunch of flowers in a vase—I couldn't help feeling a little ashamed. From flower arrangement and our hostess's skill in the art, it was them perhaps natural that we should turn to Japanese calligraphy. Baskets, vases, and special stands, which Mrs Namiwaki had used in her flower arrangements, were removed with infinite care (just as everything is always so treated in a Japanese home) and these were then replaced by fude (writing brushes), sumi (black writing ink), and paper. I could have stayed all night in such patient hospitable

Chapter 10: Happy Days with the Namiwaki's

company being taught how to write Japanese characters. All this in the peace and quiet contemplation of a Japanese home, which is what I was learning to love. What a grand day it had been; and how reluctant were Jock and I to leave, as we expressed our most sincere gratitude, and wished everyone goodbye. This was similarly matched by the many thanks, bows, and fond farewells of our hosts.

Chapter 11

Changing Times

Home by Jeep

I didn't know it at the time but that was my last visit to the Namiwaki's lovely home although, as fate would have it, I was to meet Shizue again in very different circumstances. Jock and I drove through the chill air, in his jeep, towards our camp. We did not speak. We would often enjoy each other's company in silence, almost knowing that what we were thinking about were the same things; and, in fact, we derived much mutual satisfaction from knowing just that. I was happy that I was becoming intimate with Japanese home life. I longed more and more to be invited into their homes, to learn more of their way of life, to tell them of our way, and to derive the best from them both. I thought of the months ahead, and how much more fortunate I now was than ever before. We still saw a lot of Shizue. She came to the airfield on most days, on some errand connected with her work, and she always contrived to see Jock. She also helped me to prepare a couple of speeches in Japanese which I will come to later. Jock may still have gone to Shizue's home. I do not know, but colleagues were already beginning to talk a lot about a forthcoming anti-fraternisation policy. This was all rather ambiguous; and, official guidance at the time was rather half hearted, but I felt that ultimately there was little doubt that formal directives on the subject would be issued. Jock had, I believed, been warned by various high ranking officers, who were now

Chapter 11: Changing Times

beginning to appear, that his behaviour towards the Japanese people was incorrect. He was not showing the flag, and he was considered to be mixing with local people far more than he ought to be. This was no doubt a factor in his premature posting, not very long afterwards, to the Bofu airfield where his unit was actually stationed. If Jock did go back to the Namiwaki's, he never asked me to go with him; and, after that, I never asked him. This was in loyalty to my conscience and my work, as well as to the mere thought of further frightening directives on fraternisation. For the moment, at least, I ceased to seek the wonderfully relaxing experience of Japanese family life; and I concentrated, even more fully than before, on my job.

Increasing Org. 3 workload

By this time, our work was increasing by leaps and bounds. It was becoming ever increasingly difficult to cater for the periodic and sometimes erratic arrival of troops. Jock and I spent many an evening together after dinner, working in the office. We did once, for a very short time, fall short of our one overriding instruction never to billet our troops under canvas. Just for a few days, but only for a few days, and only for a few troops—and despite all our best efforts—we failed; but, it was for a very short spell, and it happened just the once. To help the situation, I was meeting many local Japanese officials and their staff, and we worked hard to find the necessary accommodation which we needed. During the course of a day, and from these dealings, I used to get some good practice in using the Japanese language. This fortunately compensated me, momentarily, for my slackened appetite for visiting Japanese homes. My interest in Japanese family life was, of course, never far away. It did return and, by the end of my stay in Japan, I had developed an unquenchable thirst for meeting families which was almost uncontrollable. In my defence, however, I must say that my work in the office never ever faltered. It always came first and it could not have been done more conscientiously by anyone. The slight breakdown which I had shortly before leaving Japan was due in the main to sheer overwork. As I mentioned earlier, when I left Japan in September 1946, which was at a very busy time, AVM Bouchier, on his own initiative, and certainly without any prompting by myself, surprisingly wrote an excellent letter about me, to a Company to whom I was applying for employment. In it, he paid a glowing tribute to my work as "Org. 3", for which position, as he said in his letter, he had personally selected me. On the copy of his letter, which he passed on to me, he had also very kindly written a few extra kind words of good wishes.

Visiting VIPs

As time went by, we were visited by an increasing number of Very Important People (VIPs) from all over the western world. Many of them were very high ranking Military officers, Diplomats, Politicians, and Government officials. Most, if not all, were met and welcomed individually in grand style by Air Vice Marshal Bouchier, with whom they also stayed a day or so in Kikkawa house. Sometimes, they stayed longer in this splendid home which we had prepared for him. The AVM laid great store by these visits. Invariably he would decide that his visitor should be welcomed by a small military parade and a Guard of Honour, and that these should be planned down to the finest detail. I was usually required to attend the AVM's preparatory meetings for these visits, to add my views on the preparations; although, in truth, usually most of the people at the meeting had far more right to be there, than I ever had. One of the most important persons called on to help in the planning of the reception was obviously Flying Officer Bolster who was in charge of our small unit of the RAF Regiment. The unit's well disciplined welcome for all our guests was always extremely impressive and faultless, and a joy to watch. It set the right tone and ultimate success of the visits which invariably followed. Our AVM realised this, and to show his appreciation, as well perhaps his frightening power over all of us, he awarded Flying Officer Bolster immediate double promotion to the rank of acting Squadron Leader. A few of us, and at the time perhaps this also included me, thought that the AVM was possibly paying too much attention to his visitors and not enough to some of the more urgent Occupation problems. The AVM was, however, always a great believer in showing the flag, and winning the hearts and minds of those who were capable of advancing our cause. At a time, when our own UK Government had its mind perhaps on other things much nearer home than Japan, the AVM's approach was to be applauded. It undoubtedly had many hidden benefits for all of us. We had a good leader who knew what was best for us.

Chapter 11: Changing Times

Important contacts

At a local, and far less grandiose level, Jock had already wisely made contact with many, if not all, the local dignitaries in the Iwakuni area, and had made good friends of them all, often with their families as well. Jock believed that this was essential if we were to have any success in such sensitive operations as the mustering of labour, and the requisitioning of people's property. He gradually kindly introduced me to all the important local people in Iwakuni, and it was this which gave us both such influence and power. From then on, we always had at least one most influential local figure we could depend on to bring about what we wanted. I would attribute much, if not all, of our acknowledged success in our dealings with the Japanese people, to these relationships which we established. As a result, no one knew more about the local situation, how the city was run, and what was achievable and what was not, than Jock and I. That was why all enquiries came to us and to no one else. Sometime later, the anti-fraternisation policy tended to interfere with our contacts with the Japanese people. However, as I will explain later, we were often able to find ways of avoiding the policy's worst aspects. Although our small group of contacts was drawn merely from Iwakuni, or from the immediately surrounding area, they were none the less typical of the country as a whole. People from other areas, in different cities, towns, and villages up and down the country, found to an incredible degree, the same state of affairs, the same people, and the same attitudes as we did in Iwakuni. Writing now about my meetings, with these leading local dignitaries of the time, reveals the many conflicting and deeply heartfelt feelings, which we had at the time. We had to find a way of doing some extremely painful work in the most painless way we could.

Chapter 12

The local Police Chief

First encounter

The Iwakuni Police chief (Kamisugi Shochou) was a bespectacled, dark haired, nimble little man. He had a stubble chin and sallow complexion, and in western eyes was somewhat slovenly dressed, usually wearing a twisted tie; and, a mildewed trouser belt about his middle. My first encounter with him was not at all congenial. Jock and I were engaged in that ever dreaded task of evicting people in order to house some of our troops who were due to arrive the following week. We had asked for the police chief's support. Whether he was giving it unwillingly or not was difficult to tell. He seemed to operate under a mask of bland indifference and implicit obedience to do whatever we asked. We must have drawn well on his remarkable reserve of tact and patience which he was known to have. In this particular case, the owner of an old wartime decrepit factory had been served with a notice to quit and to prepare the place for our incoming troops. We had asked the Police chief to supervise the evacuation of factory personnel, and their families, from their long occupied premises. We could have enforced the eviction without any Japanese help but, to give the proceedings an air of legality, and in a true British way, we desired it to be done in as simply quiet, and as appropriately civilised, way as possible. "Chiefy", as we later always called him when we became more familiar with him, was visibly very uneasy. To whom did he owe his allegiance—to

Chapter 12: The local Police Chief

his fellow countrymen, who with their taxes paid to keep him in office; or to us, new arrivals who insisted on recruiting him into our service? There was no superior to whom he could turn for advice, no court order on which to lay the blame, and there were no specific regulations on Government procurement. They had yet to be issued by the Supreme commander. That Chiefy was able to find a way of overcoming these difficulties, of satisfying his conscience, and of remaining true to his fellow citizens, while also at the same time remaining friends with us was not easy, and was a great credit to him.

Difficult decisions

For us, on the other side of the equation, to witness the wholesale eviction of half starved, penniless, mentally and physically devastated people, to listen to them pleading to us to let them keep their last earthly possessions, was enough to turn over the strongest of stomachs. Our consciences were sorely tested. There was obviously at first no rapport between Chiefy and us. It was unpleasant. But, whatever it was that motivated him,—his sheer inability to oppose our will without resigning, or the acceptance of fate which features so much in the Japanese vocabulary, he did finally, coldly, efficiently, and with some dignity, do all which we asked him. I sometimes wondered how far I, or my fellow countrymen in England, would have helped an occupying power, as he was doing, had the tables been reversed; and, we had found ourselves under the heel of a conqueror. Chiefy's role was typical of the help which Japanese officials were prepared to give us all over the country. He knew that some of our demands would be inordinate and unjustifiable. He knew that he would be called on to perform unpleasant tasks against his own people, sometimes even taking the necessities of life from those who could least spare them. However, he was also aware that he had three children and a wife who was expecting another child to care for. The continuation of holding on to a steady job, rather than being jobless and putting up passive but ineffectual resistance, must have influenced his decision. What may have helped us in many of our cases, at least speaking for Jock and I, was that we always had the good sense to know when things were going too far; and, we did intervene when our conscience made us do so. But above all else, we were always scrupulous to show that whatever was requisitioned was never in any way for the personal benefit, either for Jock or for me. Any kindness we could possibly show to people during these dreadful occasions was also extremely helpful. Sometimes Jock and I were accompanied by the young RAF Regiment officer, Flying Officer Bill Bolster, to whom I referred earlier when writing about the furnishing of a home for our AVM, our week end parties, and parades for visiting VIPs. He had a frank and open hearted appeal for everyone. It was during one of our mad furniture grabbing raids—to a local hospital of all places—that he permitted a few quite old and frail looking medical assistants to absent themselves from the daily muster of manual labour, at the front of our HQ. News of this travelled fast and it was obviously greatly appreciated throughout the community.

Chiefy in his office

I am glad to say that all our future meetings with Chiefy were far more amicable than the first. Over time, we developed a very harmonious relationship and a spirit of mutual cooperation and trust. To sit in Chiefy's cool and inviting office, neat, clean, and spick and span, half Japanese, half western was very pleasant. As we looked around we could not but notice an obvious depletion of Chiefy's original stock of furniture, a noticeable gap just here and there which may have appeared following our earlier visits. Our Regiment officer was very impartial in his selection of whose property to procure. We would talk first about business of the day, and perhaps continue over a bottle of sake. Chiefy's deep guttural voice, approving what we asked for, was the cue for another drink. It was Chiefy who introduced me to the Japanese game of Jon, Ken, Pon, (Scissors, Stone, and Paper). If you lost, you had to take another drink. He obviously enjoyed receiving us in his own emporium and would often delight in putting on his best uniform complete with all its regalia. However he never assumed airs, or asserted undue authority over his subordinates or townsfolk. I often thought that he would have received more respect had he put on a bolder front and had a more severe manner, but then he wouldn't have been Chiefy. His attitude towards his own subordinates, however, was very much contrary to the behaviour, which I had occasionally witnessed in the city, of some of the subordinates themselves. It was not, for example, unusual to see a police officer slap a subordinate in the face several times for being untidy. In return for Chiefy's helping us, I was sometimes able to support both him and his police force, by mediating between him and one of our other outposts anywhere in the country, between him and our all powerful Provost and Military police, as well as, when required, getting him interviews at a higher level. His eventual regard for Jock and me, however, was not in any way determined by what we did for him in return. I can readily testify that Chiefy's backing and influence, on my behalf, only increased as my own powers towards the end of my tour of duty began to wane. There was one very special favour, in recovering a precious little cigarette case which I had left behind at a hotel in the country where I had stayed one weekend in the summer. He did this for me, very kindly at the end of my service in Japan, when I had much less influence than I had at the beginning. I will refer to this little episode later.

Chiefy's District interpreter

Working alongside Chiefy was an early middle aged lady named Mickey, who was working as principal interpreter for the Iwakuni district offices. She had incredible vitality and a pleasing personality and, at times, an imperious manner which earned her the nickname, General Mickey. She had a complete mastery of English and Japanese, colloquial American, undisputed knowledge of French and Spanish, and probably, like most of the English speaking girls there, a useful smattering of Hawaiian. She was now a widow, with a son about nine years old, and she had had quite a romantic history. She had been a very successful business woman and a waiting lady to a famous film star in Hollywood, and had toured the world returning to Japan just before the war. She accompanied Chiefy on almost all his visits, and was present at all meetings with the Military Government; thus acquiring more knowledge of our particular sector in Japan than any other person in it. Her power and indispensable talents became less in demand as more interpreters, both "Allied" and Japanese, presented themselves, and as officials realised the danger of one person having so much knowledge and secrets in her possession. She was suspected of trading the secrets of one side for the favours of the other, although I don't believe any case was ever brought against her. She was still holding office when I left Japan. Perhaps more importantly, than her trading of confidences, was the way sometimes, she would temper her interpretations, to make them less offensive. Unlike Shizue, she was very good at that; although, as a result, some of her exchanges were occasionally but understandably a little curt and concise. She would dispense with the flowery trimmings of her own language and ignore some of the rough and rude expressions of others in theirs which, I am sorry to say, often came from our side. Our girl interpreters on the other hand, while also wishing to avoid unpleasant expressions, often spoke too politely to men whom we wanted to admonish. The girls were of course only following the custom and rules of conduct of their own life and language. I could only concur. Chiefy and Mickey both offered a loyalty to our cause which transcended their discomfort of defeat. I had a fondness for them both, not only because involuntarily they were showing their own people the best way to accept adversity; but, also, because they were who they were. Chiefy was always Chiefy, dusty and untidy as ever. Mickey was always Mickey; whether in her drab and unbecoming European garments she wore at work, or dressed in her beautiful kimono which she also wore at other times. Leaving them at the end of my tour of duty was also the beginning of the end of my "dream Japonica", and the end of my visit to Fairyland. When I re-visited Japan in 1990 I tracked Chiefy down to a little stationers shop not far from Iwakuni city centre, which he owned, and where he was living with his daughter; but, very sadly, his daughter didn't think he was well enough to see me and to be reminded of our activities of 44 years before. It would, she said, at his age of 80+ have been far too much of a strain for him. I was so sad.

Chapter 13

AMG Liaison Officer

Mr Kawamura

Not half a mile away from Police headquarters, there was another functionary whose job was to carry out "liaison" between the American Military Government and the Japanese people. His name was Mr Kawamura, which we often used to translate as Mr Rivertown. He certainly had some influence over affairs in Iwakuni, but I was never really sure of his precise role. I also never really knew what his duties were compared, say, to those of Hank, the liaison officer in Tokyo whom I liked very much and whom I had first met in Singapore, and then again when we were jettisoning Japanese swords in the sea off Iwakuni. Hank seemed to be a roving communicator, while Kawamura San was obviously based permanently in Iwakuni; and, being Japanese, he was intended to liaise directly with local Japanese people. The arrangement so far as it impacted on us was not always as helpful as it might have been. We were not supposed to approach Mr Kawamura directly,—let alone request his services, or express a view on the effectiveness of what he was doing. If we had any complaint at all, we were asked to make it to the American Military Government, who would then censor or amend our complaint and, if suitable, pass it on to the liaison authorities, and eventually to Mr Kawamura. By his subordinates he was treated regally, but I felt that at times this attitude was a little false and affected. There was much more discipline, bowing, and enforced homage, from his civilian staff, than Chiefy would ever have expected from his people. It often pained me to be present when his subordinates waited on him and took his orders. Much to the contrary, however, his appearance was by no means commanding. He usually wore a round soft felt hat, like a schoolgirl, which topped his black dishevelled hair. This, and his dusty light grey suit which matched his hat, his rag like tie, and his brown unclean shoes, were not features which impressed people.

At work and socially

Mr. Kawamura was always saying that he regretted the "legal looting" of his furniture by the Allies which had left his office without the comforts and splendour to which his rank and position entitled him. At work it cannot be said, therefore, that he was instinctively very friendly towards us. To me personally he was always very civil; and, except in the case of one or two very difficult requisitioning issues, he was always very obliging. To be fair to Mr Kawamura, he may have felt at times that he was torn between requirements of the American Military Government and those of BCOF, which sometimes were not strictly identical. Socially, when work was forgotten, Mr Kawamura was a very different person. He was very friendly to me. On occasions, he kindly let me have the use of his car, and his chauffeur. One day, he surprisingly invited me to watch a live Japanese Sumo wrestling contest from his office window, which offered a first class view of the whole arena. It was the first time I had ever seen a Sumo wrestling match, and Mr Kawamura was obviously very delighted to have the opportunity of explaining to me, some of the niceties and intricacies of the Sport. He was, also, probably the only official in Japan of whom I ever asked a personal favour, which was to help me obtain some curtains and a chair for my room at the camp, which he very kindly did for me.

Chapter 14

The Mayor

Official relationship

My first impression of the Mayor was of a 67 year old, small, and plump, rather pot bellied gentleman, with grey hair, and white moustache, well dressed, and possessed of sufficient dignity and condescension as became his office. His hesitancy, and reluctance to fight for a given cause, could be mistaken for stubbornness, charm, helplessness, or political intrigue, depending on which school you belonged to. My usual official relationship with him arose out of his obligation to keep the Allied Forces in Iwakuni aware—through Org. 3—of any planned civic events in the city and especially of any planned visits by dignitaries from places beyond Iwakuni. It was expected that the Mayor would meet all visiting Japanese officials, excepting Commissioners of Police, which naturally was Chiefy's responsibility. The mayor then had a duty to present us with the compliments of his visitors, and If the rank and status of the visitors warranted it, to come with them in person to meet our Commander, AVM Bouchier. Jock or I would arrange this with the AOA or AOC as appropriate. The mayor, being timorous and shy, derived no joy from these visits and always asked us to make them as short as possible, if only so that he could escape the atmosphere of Allied authority which frightened him enormously. Making these arrangements might lead to my visiting him in his office in the Town Hall, or even being invited to his home.

A dubious invitation

I remember visiting the Mayor at home on one very warm summer's evening when Jock was no longer with us. I had been invited to act as interpreter along with another guest, a British Police officer who drove us there in his car. The Police officer was interested in quizzing the mayor about black marketing activity, which left me feeling a little uncomfortable; but, I had no idea at the time how serious this might turn out to be. I was determined to enjoy the evening in Japanese company. We were greeted by the mayor and after the customary removal of head and footgear by servants we were led on to a large cool veranda which seemingly overlooked a magnificent landscape, had we not known before that it was, in fact, only a miniature model. The garden was in reality just an averaged sized garden, bounded not many feet away by a terraced railway embankment. Space in Japan is cramped and valuable. Even the rich may have but a small portion of it. Before we sat down in European style deck chairs, carefully provided for us, a charming lady much younger than the mayor but apparently his wife, came and exchanged the usual salutations; and then, almost immediately, obediently disappeared. I would have preferred all feminine company to stay, but we were in for a gruelling time; and, had the mayor but known it, so was he. I resisted as long as I could attempts to engage me in the chatter. The green peaceful scenery around us was in sharp contrast to a tiring day's work in the humid climate of the Japanese summer. This for me was a haven in another world, a spot of old Japan. I had no ear for stupid worldly wiles. It was the garden which I appreciated, and which I wanted to remember. To justify my presence, I had to join the conversation at some stage, but at first I wanted to take in and enjoy the peace and quiet, pleasantly so far away from our camp. Here in this dream garden, except for a breeze, as it whistled occasionally through the bamboo trees, or rustled a few leaves, everything was so quiet and hushed. There wasn't a living sound of bird, or insect, to bring it to life.

Mayoral dinner

I would have long continued my pleasant musings but, suddenly, there was a short imperious clapping of hands; and, servants, dressed in white, and serving drinks and titbits, etc. immediately appeared, to disturb my reveries. My attention was also required as the conversation

Chapter 14: The Mayor

moved towards elections and the unsuitability and unscrupulousness of candidates. The mayor became more talkative every minute. Night descended quickly. A dark starry sky was already overhead. The air became chill and I was glad when we were invited indoors to continue our chatter over a warm meal. We went into a large room, which was more spacious than cosy, but it was still very inviting. A beautiful pillar or hashira supported the traditional toko-no-ma signifying the wealth of the family. Numerous, curious and expensive vases were carefully placed around the room. A highly polished large dark mahogany table was in the centre of the room and, on it was laid the beginnings of our evening meal. We had heard rumours of the mayor's thrift and sparing lifestyle, but here there was none of it. We were faced with a sumptuous meal of "king" rice cakes, a variety of soups and vegetables, and deliciously prepared food accompanied by sake, beer and tea. My partner, the British Police Officer, seemingly forgetting the real purpose of his visit enjoyed instead an hour of genuine Japanese hospitality. The mayor's wife had not been present while we were eating, but as we approached the tea stage, the mayor clapped his hands, and as he said a few unintelligible words, we were joined by his wife. The servants had been dismissed, so the wife's role seemed to be to continue to serve us with drinks etc.; but, in response to questions from us, she did also occasionally say a few words. Regrettably, she seemed to have the role more of a confidential servant, than a wife.

Different views on Black market activity

Our conversation proceeded rapidly, but then gradually it changed from politics and electioneering, towards a subject on which, had the mayor known it, he ought to have been more guarded in what he said. The subject was the black market, when food and goods were in short supply. The conversation may well have contributed to the mayor's later downfall. The mayor and the Police officer/detective seemed to agree that black market activity was sometimes in the interests of society! Although I tried to help in occasional translation, I remained a completely disinterested observer. I made no points of my own, and I took no part in their coming to conclusions. Later, however, as we drove homeward along the narrow winding lanes that led in bumps and mounds away from the house, I did wonder how much the mayor and Police officer had really agreed, or was the latter just trying to get the mayor's undisguised views. Personally, I had enjoyed the evening too much to worry about it. Certainly, the mayor's farewell, and the many "Please do come again" exhortations on parting, seemed particularly genuine and suggested that the mayor was very pleased with his own performance during the evening. The Police officer also possibly showed that he was no less pleased with the evening, when he admonished a poor loitering airman whom we caught out of camp at way past bedtime. His admonitory voice seemed to reflect a feeling of self righteousness. Whether the evening played any part in the mayor's later downfall I have no idea. Perhaps, I thought to myself, as we drove into our camp and as I gazed at the dark, silent, sky above with its twinkling stars, it alone would know the answer. The mayor was however later convicted for taking part in black market activity and, before I left Japan, he had in fact been sent to prison,—for which in some ways I felt very sorry—for having been, even if only very remotely, connected with his story.

Chapter 15

The City Headmaster

School curricula overturned

Iwakuni's headmaster was the head of a large important secondary school which had many teachers with a wide variety of skills. I used to see him at the school and also at the Iwakuni Cultural Society of which he was a committee member. I always addressed him as Sensei (literally meaning a teacher or scholar, but it is also an honorific indicating my appreciation and respect both for him and for his academic achievements). He was a tall, well built, upright man in his mid forties, strong and firm in body as he was in purpose. He had penetrating eyes and a grim steady smile which reflected a welcome stability in a country which at that time was still wavering, jittery, and a little jumpy. The more I saw of him, the more I understood and liked him, and especially I liked the approach he was taking in very difficult times, to his teaching work. He was moving as it were in a world of pitfalls, aware of having previously been duped and deceived, but he was now determined not to make the same mistakes again. The volte face in the school's teaching syllabus, since the arrival of the Allies, and the very direct supervision to which all schools in Japan had previously been subject, might well have left a man of less finer mettle than he was, completely distraught. However, he had laboriously studied the problem; had admitted earlier mistakes; and was now concentrating for all his worth on a healthier and more truthful future. Hitherto, real responsibility for education had been entirely with the State, and its ministers. A school could do little about teaching English and certain other subjects, when these were banned as they were during the war. He could not, at that time, have disputed the authenticity of distorted geography and history text books, which had been prescribed for his school, any more than he could have denied the divinity of the Emperor, or the fantastic decrees and exhortations published in the latter's name. However, now at least, he was free to teach the truth, as he saw it, and not as it was laid down by some bureaucrat. Freedom of thought had in one sense been restored. The future depended on the attitude, and competence of himself and his colleagues in how they managed the changes. It cannot be denied that much of Japan's future success had its roots in the excellent efforts of teachers like "Sensei".

Iwakuni's School

I visited Iwakuni's school usually when they were expecting a visit by an Allied Education officer. However, at any time and for any visitor, it was always an impressive occasion. The school building was made almost completely of wood but otherwise it followed fairly closely the construction of any large western school. It was beautifully clean, and the floors were polished like mirrors, due to the splendid attention of the pupils who were on a roster to do the daily charring. Whereas, at home, the children of the school might never see a chair; here, in each school classroom, there were at least 50 desks, and far more than 50 chairs and stools. Some desks may have had to make room for more than one occupant but at least there was no squatting on the floor, and students had somewhere to write down their lessons. Each classroom, although a little large for practical purposes, was spacious and healthy. Ceilings were at least 25 feet high. There were pleasant concrete playgrounds and a large sports field close by. In short, as a place of learning, and with slightly fewer pupils, it would have rated highly compared with any first class school in the West. Sensei had good reason to be proud of it.

Bewilderment

Given the grave post war situation at the time, the children were reasonably happy; but, they could be forgiven their bewilderment, both at the changes in their curriculum and the new direction in which they were now being taught. The very trying conditions in which they were expected to study, the malnutrition in their diet, the need for overcrowding, sometimes two pupils to a desk, one half of the class working in the mornings and the other half in the afternoon, were all undoubtedly taking their toll. It could not be expected that such children, many of them poorly fed, ill clad, and probably with thoughts of having to work after school in the black market, would be able to give their undivided attention to what their masters were teaching them. But, to the credit of Sensei, he never criticised his pupils. He made proper allowances and always praised them for the efforts which they were making against all the odds. Understandably, I always refrained from asking what might be considered meddlesome and embarrassing questions. I wondered, for example, why the pupils, as if from habit rather than need, walked on the hard wooden floors in bare or stockinged feet, while masters and mistresses wore straw sandals. The school flooring had been built to Western design. It was not made of tatami, or closely woven straw, as it was in the student's homes. Another topic which sometimes made me feel a little uncomfortable was teacher-student relationship. In general, I had great respect for the order and quiet studious atmosphere of Japanese schools. It contrasted sharply with the rowdiness sometimes found in some Western schools, but at times it did seem to me that Sensei's students often showed excessive deference (almost servility) towards their teachers. The youngest teacher there, a young girl, perhaps only 18 or 19 years old, seemed to have as much power and control over her charges, who were sometimes only slighter younger than herself, as a general over his troops. While due deference and respect are certainly valued, and required from all students, they should also certainly be encouraged to do their own thinking, to ask questions, and frequently to put forward opposing views to established ideas. It was all of course a matter of balance and how it was done.

Allied Forces' interest

It could hardly be expected that all the teaching staff, even under the brilliant leadership of Sensei, would take kindly to their new conditions. Members of staff were no longer the symbols of higher authority and puppets of the state, passing on a political message. They were now individual teachers, who were expected to take the initiative in bringing out the best in children, encouraging them to study, to ask questions, and at times even to question established beliefs. How children were taught would have a big effect on their lives and the future of the country. Sensei realised this. He believed in Western policies and also that the future of Japan lay in the hands of teachers like himself. Without Sensei's guidance, many of his staff may well have floundered. It is possible that a few of Sensei's staff still preferred the old regime, and did not want to give up the sense of power and authority, which they had once exercised on behalf of the State. It was on this very point that I felt the Americans and ourselves may have done more to help him. On the other hand, it was not of course a primary duty of an occupying power to re-develop a country's educational system.

A good intention goes wrong

Sometimes, Sensei would invite us to attend a class which he was teaching. On one occasion, my companion, the Allied Government's Education officer, was asked if he would take over an English lesson. The class was delighted to have two live real English guinea pigs on whom to practice their use of this weird language which had until recently been banned but was now again in favour. Unfortunately the student's joy was merged quickly with dismay. My companion had started to read from a text book, speaking in a broad Scottish accent, which even I found difficult to follow. The pupils fidgeted uneasily, and Sensei was even more perplexed. He rose to take over the class again. As we left, rather sheepishly, very shortly afterwards, we could hear a voice saying in comically Pidgin English, "Ze bai's name is a Jaku. Jaku has a brusa.". Sensei was however nodding approvingly, and he waived to us as we passed out of view. Unfortunately, no one had thought of the little difficulty of speaking in an English lesson with a Scottish accent and Scottish pronunciation.

Unhelpful actions by Allied Forces

Perhaps more harmful than this were sometimes the sudden "educational visits" in search of seditious teaching, and the snooping by some officials to prevent what was believed (even for those times) to be excessive punishments in schools. The "visits" were said to ensure a proper scholastic and academic environment, but in fact at times

Chapter 15: The City Headmaster

the visitors seemed to be more like watch dogs, looking for wrong doing. If it had been possible, visits by confidential advisers from Allied countries, or even representatives from the United Nations, free from political taint, would have done more good than these official police-like actions, which were not only unhelpful, but strongly resented. Possibly, there was a belief in some quarters, that schools could still be used to pass on political doctrine, as it had been so used in the past, but surely there were better ways of preventing this. In modern Japan, teachers needed to be aware that they were not political tools of anybody. They should always avoid any chance of their being used in this way. One subject, which I loved to see being taught anywhere in Japan, was Japanese calligraphy, or the writing of Japanese characters. Most Japanese scholars were brilliant and expert at this, writing beautiful characters, carefully, and gracefully, examples of which I was often given and keep to this day. It is a cultural heritage. But, even here, persuasive slogans and sentences like "Minshu Shugi—Nihon Saikin"—"Japan will be re-built on democracy" were often chosen—reminding us of the care which is always needed to be impartial. On another day and in very different circumstances, a totally different example might easily be used,—depending on the fashion of the times. Another unhelpful measure, for good relationship between peoples and especially children, which came into effect about half through my stay in Japan, to which I will be referring later, was the Allied government's regrettable attitude to fraternisation. Despite these issues, and sometimes differing points of view, Sensei and I were always the best of friends. He was always very glad to see me, and always made me very welcome at his school. I could only believe that this sincere warmth between us was again a wonderful part of the amazingly good fortune which accompanied me throughout the whole of my stay in Japan.

Chapter 16

The Miyazaki's—Another Wonderful Family!

Emiko

    Undoubtedly, the best of very many good turns which Jock did for me was to introduce me to Emiko and, a little later, to her family, the Miyazaki's. Emiko was a very pretty girl of about twenty or twenty one, of fair complexion, beautifully shiny black hair, with a full, attractive, figure and an extremely pretty face. She had been doing domestic work at the airfield since our occupation, and had been spotted by Jock as "superior". It was to him that she eventually devoted most of her time. Jock, as I have indicated, was a power in the land and highly respected by all Iwakuni citizens. Emiko was perhaps therefore not a little proud to be his guardian samurai. Her devotion to Jock was I am sure no less than that of the Chushingura in Japan's medieval history. The loyalty and devotion to us, of all the girls who waited on us at the camp, was likewise never in question. Emiko had had a very good education in a country where education was highly rated and, for which to pay for, parents were often prepared to suffer considerable hardship. She had graduated among a few from a local girl's high school and had gained a confidence from it which only education can give. Examination standards were particularly high;—sometimes with as many as seven students out of eight failing to get a first grade pass.

Chapter 16: The Miyazaki's—Another Wonderful Family!

Emiko also had a natural talent for playing the koto, the samisen, and other Japanese musical instruments, from which I was destined to derive much future enjoyment. It was my friendship with this family, and its personal warmth which, more than anything else sustained my fondness for Japan during the remainder of my service time which I spent there. They left me with some of my fondest memories. Together, the Namiwaki's and the Miyazaki's gave me the intimate knowledge of Japanese family life for which I had been thirsting.

An unscheduled visit

It must have been only about two weeks before he left for Bofu, when Jock told me that he and a friend of his, who was moving to Bofu with him, had spent a very happy evening with the Miyazaki's. They had been invited there again that evening, but his friend couldn't make it. Would I accept the invitation and go in place of his friend? At first, I didn't really want to take the place of someone who had actually received the invitation. It did not seem fair on the Miyazaki's, who would be expecting Jock's friend, and who were also no doubt preparing a true Japanese welcome for him. It wouldn't show me in a very fair light, and I would be the centre of their disappointment from the beginning. I would appear, not as a proper guest, but someone unknown, uninvited, and possibly unwanted. However, I had not visited Shizue for more than a fortnight. My desires and longing to delve further into Japanese family life and customs was stronger than ever. I felt that I just couldn't refuse. This feeling—coupled with Jock's inimitable persuasion—would have been strong enough to take me anywhere. Nevertheless, I continued to think how awkward I would be when I arrived, and I was worried whether I would be able to explain myself in Japanese, and how stupid I would seem trying to explain myself in imperfect Japanese. It hadn't occurred to me that Jock had already given the Miyazaki's all necessary explanation, very successfully. I would be seen as a young conceited officer who had intruded, unwanted, over their threshold. I thought I would be a skeleton at the feast, and very probably captious, and ready to carp at anything. It was not an auspicious beginning.

Harmony is irresistible

Fortunately, I recovered completely. This was due largely to what I had already learned about true Japanese family life. I realised that if I was prepared to enter Japanese homes, especially in the face of laws now being drawn up against it, there were no half measures. I would have to go as a fully fledged friend or not at all. I had to enter into the spirit of the occasion, as Jock had always done. In accepting the Miyazaki's hospitality, I decided that I had to be on my best behaviour and not at all formal. The Miyazaki family would then respond as Japanese families always seemed to do. Their friendly solicitations, their desire for harmony and warm greeting, would put me at ease, and I would soon be a member of a very happy circle. These thoughts coaxed me gently back into a better humour. This was the same stoical behaviour of Japanese people which often relieved the pain and concern of others; but, which also, sometimes, concealed their own grief and troubles. It was the kind of stoicism which I admired. Americans, and to a lesser extent Europeans, in their communications, were generally more outspoken and frank than the Japanese. Such expressions could sometimes hurt, often for no real purpose. Japanese people, to the contrary, realised that very candid remarks could be thoughtless, brutal and, later, very often regretted. In the home especially, Japanese people preferred to follow "Wa, Wa-hei, and Wa-go" (harmony, peace, and unity). These are splendid Japanese words for these qualities, but the meanings of them are sometimes difficult to convey in English. Japanese people fully understood them, however; and, the kanji for them were very often very carefully drawn, and displayed about the home. Both visitors and family would see these kanji and be reminded of their value. It was quite common, I had been told, for families displaying these kanji to hold regular meetings, at which all members of the family, especially large families (and no matter what their ages) would attend. They would all sit on cushions around the large general purpose table of the family, and discuss their family's problems and plans which might affect each other. Such family gatherings were a wonderful expression of family unity, and really a delight to imagine. (Many years later, I found that such activities were depicted in films, in television drama, and in other media of the time. I didn't have to imagine them; they were obviously very real and true). But, suddenly, Jock had stopped and parked the jeep in which we were travelling. We were just a few feet away from

Chapter 16: The Miyazaki's—Another Wonderful Family!

the Miyazaki's cycle shop. It was dusk. Eventide was almost upon us. I could barely make out the form and shape of the nearby buildings, or even the bridge ahead, which, as usual, was busy with traffic. However, by now, it was not the noise and bustle of the streets of Iwakuni which were foremost in my mind; but, rather, the very inviting and friendly harmony of a Japanese home.

A magical entrance

Jock and I made our way quietly into the Miyazaki's garden, entering it through a typically arched gateway with its attractively latticed, but rather well worn, garden gate resting beneath it. We immediately found ourselves walking down a lovely little garden path towards the house. Although I didn't know it then, it was a path with which I was to become very familiar, and one which I was to tread on many similar occasions, in the weeks and months to come. My heart raced ahead, missed a beat, and began to beat even faster; as it did, even more noticeably, on future visits. It was an intense, almost indescribable, feeling, as I wondered what was in store for me in the evening ahead. The Miyazaki's would certainly have been intrigued had they known my feelings. We moved on into a small inner yard, and then on to a veranda of the house. Here, we sat down on a raised and well polished floor, which projected from the house at a height of about two feet above the ground; and, on which we sat, and removed our shoes. We rang the bell in order to announce our arrival, and awaited the coming of our hosts. Emiko was dressed in a beautiful silk kimono, which took my breath away, and her mother was dressed in an equally fine kimono but of a much more sober colour. After a few introductory remarks, Jock and I were ushered into a cosy little room located two rooms back from the entrance. We had arrived.

A typical Japanese room

It was not as warm a room as we might have expected in the West. Few Japanese rooms were then really that warm in winter and early spring. There were no upholstered armchairs into which one could snuggle, no carpets or heavy curtains with their clinging warmth; but, for all that, it was a very attractive room and a part of the Japan which I had longed to see. It was like a doll's house, or a "Meccano" toy with many standard parts, each with its own interesting story. In the far

Memoires of Japan 1946

right hand corner of the room, standing majestically and commanding the whole scene, was the imposing well polished butsudan, or Buddhist altar. This was the family shrine, and to judge by the carefully arranged flowers at its base, and its spotlessly clean condition, I imagined that it had the earnest and most dutiful respect of all the family. To the left of the Butsudan, and reaching to the other wall, there was the famous tok-no-ma, a relic of the past, but in the distant past it had been a part of every Japanese home without exception. Literally, the meaning of toko-no-ma is a space for a bed. It is an attractive recess of about two feet in depth, which is built into the structure of the house. The base of the toko-no-ma is wooden and raised about six inches above the "tatami", which is a very evenly woven, smooth, base of straw matting with which all Japanese floors used to be made. In olden times, when the floors were often merely earth, the toko-no-ma provided both a bed space and comparative protection from small life which existed in the soil. Symbolically, the toko-no-ma is still a very important place of a home; and, for a guest to be invited to sit in front of it, with his or her back facing the toko-no-ma, it is a place of honour. In the Miyazaki's toko-no-ma, there were two alcoves. The first of these, at the right of the toko-no-ma, was a decorative alcove containing a very pretty hanging scroll which was then called a kakemono, but is now called a kakejuku. The scroll displayed a favourite family landscape. Sometimes it contained the words of wisdom of some famous person, or paintings of birds and flowers, and so on. Below this, there was a small stand on which was placed an artistic ornament. At first, this seemed to me to be a grotesque combination of an elephant and a dinosaur, which had been wrought in a heavy lead like metal. It was quite frightening. Happily for me, I noticed in later visits, that it had been replaced by a much more pleasing arrangement of flowers. In the left alcove of the toko-no-ma, at the left hand side, there were two small upper cupboards and one lower one made up of neat, stretched out panels or shelves, rather like a letter H on its side;—the lower part of the letter H, not quite reaching the right side of the alcove, and the higher part of the letter H not quite reaching the left. Standing upright between the two alcoves, there was a dividing pillar known as the toko-bashira, which is a very expensive piece of wood, sometimes knotted and beautifully gnarled. Sometimes, as it was at the Miyazaki's, it is plain; but it is always highly polished.

Chapter 16: The Miyazaki's—Another Wonderful Family!

A new world

I was in a new world. Jock sat in the place of honour in front of the toko-no-ma; and, later, when I went there without Jock, I was always invited to sit there. A neat dark table of polished mahogany was placed in front of Jock; and, on it, ash trays, matches, cigarettes etc. Beside him, and next to me, there was a hibachi, or globular marble bowl of burning charcoal, which was to be our fire. Sometimes a quilt is placed over the hibachi and the family get warm by sitting round it, with each member of the family being allowed to cover their knees or, with consent of the others, to tuck in their hands as well. We had no need to resort to that on this occasion. All this possibly sounds primitive now, but it was typically Japanese at that time; and the Japanese people loved it, cherishing the old ways of their ancestors. Such conservatism, in a country remarkably radical, was an example of the sometimes strange Japanese temperament. There was no other furniture in the room. Instead of chairs, we sat on some very soft brown coloured cushions which had been placed out for us on the floor around the room. The fusuma (or sliding doors to the room) were kept closed to keep in the heat of two hibachi. Hot tea was placed before us and we soon became tolerably warm and talkative. I was literally in another world. I had been in a Japanese home before with Shizue and her family, but I was already feeling at home in this new company. It may also have been due to the Miyazaki's persistent kindness in the face of my initial awkwardness. I remember particularly lying back on my elbows, stretching my legs, and feeling an attachment to the Miyazaki's, which no force could resist. Jock guessed my feelings by my changed attitude and demeanour. Socially, perhaps the Miyazaki's were not as high in the scale as was Shizue's family. However, Emiko's father was a successful farmer and businessman, as well as the owner of a cycle repair shop and the local cinema. He had made his own way in the world travelling from Hawaii when Emiko was tiny, and he was probably as comfortable now as the average Japanese family expected to be. The Namiwaki's, on the other hand, sometimes seemed a little uncomfortable, and perhaps out of their depth, in the now different world around them. The father of the family had been an important railway director and business man in pre-war Japan, but he had died during the war years. Although he had left money and property, the Occupation's terms were severe, and all unearned income was restricted to a very small figure per month. The family were living at a standard far below that which they had been used to. They were undoubtedly finding life if not difficult then very strange. It was inevitable that I would find interest in a family, perhaps a little more at ease with itself. The Namiwaki's were of course always the perfect hosts, and meticulously attentive to the pleasures of their guests. If the anti-fraternisation laws had not been introduced, and if the Namiwaki's home had not been so difficult to get to, there is no doubt I would have visited them until my last few days in Japan. My interest in them was not so much in their home, as in their charming and splendid selves.

The evening's entertainment

Here, in Emiko's happy circle, I felt that my cravings to know more of Japanese home life would be satisfied. Emiko did not have the diffidence and lack of confidence which at that time characterised Shizue. Emiko still had the charm and gentleness of all Japanese women, but she also had the courage to state her own views. She would engage in a very logical and interesting conversation. She would give me her own true opinions about present Japan, and was not to be constrained by the day's circumstances; and, not at all, by the fact that she was talking to someone of the opposite sex. My first evening at her home, however, was not to be spent discussing political or economic problems, or even the intriguing history of Japanese social life. I was the second guest, and I could hardly re-arrange the evening which had been planned. Having overcome any possibly instant dislike of me, the Miyazaki's wanted to know more about me. They gave me scope to talk and regain my ease and natural self. Then, the limelight moved back to Jock. At Jock's invitation, Emiko moved behind him, to take what seemed to me to be like a Graf Zeppelin, which was wrapped in a light bright cover of floral design, and which was resting against the lovely hanging scroll in the toko-no-ma. It was however not an airship, nor a weapon. It was something much more delicate.

Introduction to the "koto"

When uncovered, the mystery bulk eventually turned out to be one of my favourite musical instruments. It was about six feet in length, and had a base of solid wood, grained and well polished, on which 13 strings were mounted each of them supported by a little bridge to

Chapter 16: The Miyazaki's—Another Wonderful Family!

keep the string stretched and taut. It was the "koto", about which I had heard so much. Emiko placed it diagonally across the right corner of the room, facing towards Jock and me, with the toko-no-ma behind us. Her mother, who was obviously very pleased at what her daughter was about to do for us, sat at Emiko's right facing Jock. Emiko, carefully putting the ivory rings on her fingers in order to be able to pluck the strings of the koto, then placed a mass of jumbled characters and hieroglyphics on to a stand in front of the koto. She sat down gracefully, tuned the instrument for a few minutes, explained the title of the music, and began to play. The piece was called the "Song of the "Pluvver", and although I can't claim to have fully understood it, I was absolutely fascinated. I felt extremely privileged to be enjoying, first hand, in really admirable surroundings, such a fine rendition of the song. I clapped enthusiastically, upon which Emiko began to play another piece; this time, in a soft, clear, voice, also beautifully singing the words. By now, I was beyond the realm of music. Everything seemed so gentle, soothing, and tender. I wandered into the realm of dreams. This was a simplicity and beauty which, before, I had only read about. Such a scene may, I imagined, have happened once upon a time in Victorian England; but, if so, we had now lost the knowhow. Here, was a lovely peaceful room, gently lit, simply furnished, a pretty girl in a pretty dress, instrument and music, deep thoughts, absolute contentment, a couple of very grateful guests, and above all a happy parent trying, hard but in vain, to conceal her irrepressible but justifiable pride! It was a scene more beautiful than all that which the clamorous world outside had to offer. Here was something so much more valuable to find in the home itself. Jock, now perhaps beyond my age of dreams and youthful philosophy, was fidgeting, and not so much moved as I was. He lit a cigarette and Emiko reluctantly made as if to put her instrument aside; but, as ever in his own inimitable style, Jock rapidly saved the situation. He suggested that Emiko should play two tunes before she finished. One was entitled the "Song of the firefly" which had the same tune as "Auld Lang Syne"; and the other was the well known western tune, "Coming through the Rye". Emiko re-acted immediately, adjusted the bridges holding up the strings of the koto, and re-tuned them to suit the western music. The oriental strain which remained made the Koto sound all the more enchanting. We all joined together in humming the tunes. Our faces brightened up and our hearts swelled with warmth. We sang the songs again and again, breaking into lots of laughter between the pauses. Emiko was acknowledged to be truly a master, and she put away the koto;—a very happy girl.

Unstoppable time

More tea came on to the scene, and the clock in the next room ticked away merrily but also very sadly made us aware of the relentless passage of time. Time was so precious. If only we could hold it still; but that was not to be. Father and brother (Miyazaki San and his son) appeared to say good evening and to be introduced to us. There was some friendly banter between us and general bonhomie discussion, but they didn't stay for long. We were soon again, Mrs Miyazaki, Emiko, Jock, and me. With the fresh warm tea, our blood circulated more quickly, thoughts came back to us, and our tongues wagged. Somehow the subject veered to the ritual of Western marriage. Before long, Jock was kneeling next to Emiko, arms linked singing "here come the bride". He said I was best man and so I should kiss the bride. I was amazed that Jock should be so thoughtless as to bring up such a sensitive subject with Japanese people as kissing; but evidently our hosts knew him better than I did, and our merriment continued, but not the kiss. It was raining hard when the clock in the next room struck eleven. We began to say goodnight to each other. Mother and daughter carrying large umbrellas escorted us to our jeep we had parked outside three hours or so before. Jock still had the audacity, despite changing times, to use his jeep on evening visits and to leave it parked outside a house in Iwakuni's main street. Later, I was much more circumspect. The jeep took a long time to start, and we got soaking wet, but I didn't notice the rain soaked seat on which I sat beside Jock watching as Emiko and her mother waved affectionately, crying out so sweetly "Come again please", "Do come again please".

A private talk with Jock

Jock drove us hurriedly back to camp, out of the main street and into the muddy bumpy lane, which led past the Relief Society whose building we had failed to requisition the other day, across the flooded paddy fields, past the sentry at the gate, and pulled up at the back of the Mess now in complete darkness. "Come up for a drink" he shouted

Chapter 16: The Miyazaki's—Another Wonderful Family!

and after returning my hat and mackintosh to my room I joined him in his. We drank and looked back—myself, over the last five unbelievable weeks; and he, as far back as early January, seven weeks before that. I suppose we had both known for some time that, sooner or later, Jock would have to rejoin his unit in Bofu; but, now, the reality was here and on top of us. "Well," Jock said "It is all up to you now. I've introduced you to all I know and to some remarkable families. Your contacts are made. Make the best of them!" I sighed and threw back my head. I didn't think I would ever be capable of making such visits without Jock. After all, I had been a mere follower of Jock. Wherever we went, it was he who was feted. I just came in for the crumbs at the feast. He looked at my disconsolate and negative shrug. "Oh yes you will" he said. "But what about you, Jock, isn't all this just going to be devastating for you "Yes" he said "I wish I were staying on. I shall miss Emiko. She has been a guardian angel for me, tireless, and clever". I believed him; I really felt sorry for him, and even sorrier for him than I did than for myself. But still; I did also wonder, just what Jock's departure would mean for me. I knew that I already more than just liked Emiko. I knew that Emiko was intending to leave the camp with some other girl friends as soon as Jock left, but I also knew that Jock was my only means of keeping in touch with her. I could only sigh, wonder, and wait.

In India, Lt Aizawa (second from the left), the author behind him, plus four comrades and the driver—Chapter 1.

The dreadful remains of Hiroshima—Chapter 3.

Hank (seated)—the RAF Squadron Leader with an American voice—with the Author—Chapters 2 & 5.

Hank returning with us after disposing
of swords at sea—Chapter 5.

Fusae San.
Room girl for Author and Jack Evans—Chapter 5.

Early days—"Patrol" in the Inland Sea—Chapter 5

Iwakuni's *famous Golden Bridge—the Kintai bashi*
postcard of the bridge in 1946 Chapters 9, 18, & 30

Author at his desk in HQ BCAir Iwakuni—Chapter 5.

A home fo the AVM—Air Vice Marshal Bouchier's home in Iwakuni—Chapter 5.

Iwakuni's *famous Golden Bridge – the Kintai bashi*

Photograph of the original 1946 scroll which still hangs proudly in the author's home today. Chapters 9, 18 & 30

AVM Bouchier greets Sir Alvary Gascoigne,
First Political Representative in Japan in 1946. Chapter 11.

Emiko Miyazaki—playing the Samisen Chapter 16

Emiko Miyazaki—playing the koto—Chapter 16.

Souvenirs galore. Iwakuni Main Street—Chapter 18

Mark Maclaughlin, Jack Evans (the author's room mate) and Fujimoto San, at one of her famous Tea Ceremonies.—Chapter 21

Captain Brown (centre) RAA BCAIR Transport Officer,
Flying Officer Patel (Indian Liaison) and the author (right). Chapter 27.

Aizawa San, in his ship in New York Harbour in 1946,—now
the Chief Executive and Captain of a ship belonging to
the prestigious Nihon Yu-sen Kaisha—Chapter 30

Iwakuni's *famous Golden Bridge—the Kintai bashi*
A close up view and a fond last look

The whole of BCAIR—outside HQ—has been
built up to its maximum strength

Our job is complete

CHAPTER 17

GOOD BYE TO JOCK AND THE END OF AN ERA

BCAIR's first most valuable asset

Jock and I had worked steadily, day by day together, on basic administration, looking after our troops, building up our forces and meeting their requirements. We also responded quickly to requests which came from BCOF HQ in Kure, or from any of our four Air Services way back in the UK, Australia, New Zealand, or India. Then, at the end of the first week in April, for me at least—calamity! Jock, the idol of all the Japanese servants, girls and men, the father of us all, was given notice to quit. Strictly, he had never been a member of BCAIR HQ; and so, finally, he was being transferred back to his home base in Bofu. But, without him, Iwakuni would never be the same. Squadron Leader Jock Ogilvie had been the most valuable asset of our headquarters. He had laid the foundation of BCAIR from early 1946, when there were only a few Australians in Iwakuni; and, at that time, no one here from the UK at all. With a sincere and common sense approach to the huge task that awaited us, Jock had built up a very healthy relationship with the local population. If there were knots to untie, Jock was the one man who could untie them. Not for nothing, was he called King of the Castle and Squire of the City. It goes without saying that if there was ever anything difficult to be done Jock was always able to arrive at a reasonable conclusion. With unsparing help from Jock, I learned much from his ways with which I was usually in instinctive accord. Together, we had a lot of influence over events in both Iwakuni and BCAIR; but, rather than promoting our own ideas, in most cases we were really spokesmen for higher graces. At work and play, Jock and I became inseparable. Our disappearance from the mess after dinner, about 6 pm each evening, was the source of much amusement. "They are off again—where were you two last night?" was a favourite taunt of our mess colleagues. Jock would drive me round the city; and introduce me to this person or that. He had been my passport to popularity. I had been his friend and was heralded as his successor; but I feared I would make a poor second. There were so many things which he had started, both officially and socially. I knew that I would try my hardest to continue to make my stay in Japan a very happy and adventurous experience. But, it was a sad, sad, day, for me when Jock finally departed.

No final farewell party

Probably due to our evening wanderings, and to Jock not broadcasting news of his departure, there was no party or official send off for him. I felt it should have been quite a big affair but he would be the last person to suggest one; and he went off unheralded and almost unnoticed. The next morning I was asked many times, "Where's Jock? Has he got a hangover?" On reflection, it was perhaps a good time for Jock to leave us. He would never have retained his position as the benevolent lord of the manor for much longer; he would have become no more than his rank; and his often incautious but frank fraternising might have led him into trouble, even if it had not already expedited his departure. When he left, however, it was like losing an important part of me. I had known him but seven weeks but, during that time, work and our common interests and beliefs had cemented a firm friendship. Thank heaven that, for some time afterwards, I was able speak with him each day over the telephone, and tell him the local news. Sometimes I arranged for him to visit us, but gradually our contacts grew less and less frequent, and he became a distant friend to be talked about; and, in time, a very happy memory. He was the first Australian with whom I had ever made friends. He had been born in Scotland (in 1895, strangely in the same year as AVM Bouchier). He was also, to my mind a true and perfect representative of his adopted country.

Chapter 17: Good Bye To Jock and The End of an Era

Fraternisation

When Jock landed in Japan in January 1946, and I arrived nearly two months later, neither of us had ever heard about any such thing as a policy forbidding the fraternising with Japanese nationals. In fact the disposition of both of us was to do exactly that. Our AOA, in his interview with us, had never made any mention of a fraternisation policy, and nothing indeed was further from our minds. If the reason for imposing a ban on fraternising was to attribute blame for the horrible effects of war, this was a matter being dealt with by an International court; and, in a wider sense, History would be the judge. As to which country or countries were guilty of committing the worst atrocities in the conflict, and of causing the most suffering to people, this again was not easy question to answer and, in any case, not one for us. Blame can never be put on an entire nation, or on every single person in it. The simple fact before us was that Japan was now in dire trouble; and its peoples were suffering terrible hardships. The approach of the Japanese people was to take the shock of it all very bravely; to live their lives as normally as possible; to retain their traditions and customs, from which they gained both solace and strength; and, fortunately for us, to have no desire to resist the Occupation. It was no more than an act of simple humanity that we, while presently in charge of things, should help the country to get back on its feet and become again a respectable, respected, nation. We tried to do that job. It was a very difficult job to do and it required the cooperation of the Japanese people. Any ban on talking to them, exchanging views with them, and to some extent also socialising with them, made the job almost impossible; or, in any case, very much harder.

From rumours to facts

At first, rumours were flying around that a fraternising ban was being considered and plans had been drawn up in draft in Kure. Views in this direction were even being expressed by authorities in the UK, Australia, New Zealand, and India; but nothing in them seemed really firm or concrete, and so we generally ignored them. Eventually, however, tentative, and later more permanent, directives came across my desk which I naturally had to pass on. But, even these notices seemed sometimes rather half hearted,—or was this perhaps a little bit of my wishful thinking? As I found on my visit to Tokyo later, even

Memoires of Japan 1946

General MacArthur (in Chapter 25) had been quoted on the matter as saying that "it would be better for Nature to take its course". Even by the time I left Japan, when the instructions against fraternisation were in full force, there is no doubt that many a blind eye was being taken against breaches of the policy. In discussions with members of the legal branch many years later, I gathered that the legal branch itself had thought that the Allies fraternisation policy in Japan was generally misguided. The policy, it was said, was aimed not so much against genuine friendliness, but specifically against black market operations which were reaching gigantic proportions. It was also aimed at reducing widespread prostitution in the Forces, the so-called Red light situation, illicit sexual intercourse, and all its consequences. Conversation with people with whom we were doing official business was obviously excluded from the ban, as were general exchanges and enquiries, but social gatherings and visits to private homes were obviously taboo. Sometimes, some officers, for example from the legal branch doing their normal work, and others like myself, who had been requested by the British Council to attend and give lectures on the British Way of Life, had a special dispensation to meet and mix with Japanese people. In my case, I would have found it extremely difficult not to visit families with whom I had been friendly from long before the ban. I managed to continue my visits discreetly and with very great care. I was never subjected to any investigation on the matter, and I have fortunately been able to keep in contact with many of these families to the present day. My secret was never, in any way, to be seen as flaunting disrespect for the law. Jock may have found this more difficult than I did.

CHAPTER 18

WALKABOUTS IN IWAKUNI

Fortitude in misfortune

While Jock was with us in Iwakuni, my visits outside the camp were usually to do with work. In the evening, socially, my visits were to families like the Namiwaki's, the Miyazaki's, and other interesting people whom I have yet to mention. With Jock's departure, I also began evening strolls in and around Iwakuni, which lasted on and off until the end of September, when I left Japan. Sometimes I would be alone and sometimes with a friend. I would walk around the city, down into the High street and into the back streets, longing to capture and retain forever the far eastern flavour of living which was all around me. It was something I felt I might never have the opportunity to capture again—not only the exotic sense of place and its landscape, but of the people and their views. I was able to catch a momentary glimpse of that very early post war scene and the very trying and harsh conditions which had at first obtained. Japan would certainly be on show in the future—not for troops but for tourists. But, never again, would her fortune be at such low ebb and at a time when she was so desperately and unwittingly showing her all. Her people were defenceless and resigned to their fate. There was no longer any martial spirit of the samurai, pretence, or fear of losing face, with which Japan had previously been associated. Now, the Japanese people were purely themselves in their own surroundings. They were frank, friendly, and natural in their conduct and, for many of us, surprisingly warm in their welcome. As time ticked by, there was one remarkable trait which I sensed was developing and which redounded greatly to their credit. I. Gradually, as they shook off their despair, they recovered. They were not at all broken in spirit. They clung to their traditions and customs, and their way of life. They picked themselves up; and, by sheer will power and working hard, they became determined to succeed. As summer approached, I would often see and hear Japanese people in their homes, or in their sheds at the bottom of their gardens, working late into the night making products to sell or to barter. We called these hard working people, hataraki bachi (working bees or workaholics). After the terrible shocks they had suffered, people it is true were bowed; but, they were by no means broken. They had a devotion to work which later would lead them into a golden age of economic prosperity (sai-sei-ki), which earned them the admiration and envy of the world.

A bridge to reality

Most of my solitary walkabouts in Iwakuni, as well as those which I occasionally made with a friend, were in the evening after I had eaten. I would walk down the rain ruined road from our camp in Iwakuni, say on a hot summer's evening, dodging pools and pot holes, listening to the deafening croaks of frogs in the bordering rice fields on either side of me. Thinking of the wonderful fortune that had brought me there, I would shrug off any daytime concerns. I would mend my pace and walk briskly to my nightly goal. Each time when I went along that highly banked and ill-kept road, I came to "my city". The path I journeyed along came to a bridge. It was not the famous Iwakuni Golden Bridge (or Kintai bashi), with its beautiful five spans stretching picturesquely across the lovely Nishiki River towards the green hills beyond the city. No, it was a more every day, practical structure, which by day carried heavy military traffic from the camp and by night was lost in darkness. For me, the bridge I was crossing was like a bridge between two kinds of life. In one life, I was in the office in which I was very, very, happy doing what I did. I was certainly privileged to be dealing with such fascinating problems; but it was still formal work, which followed established rules and practices which are found in most stable communities. The other life was one which I craved to know more about. It was to get a peep into their raison d'être and how they were coping in their very difficult times. On the right, just before the bridge, there was a small cycle shop which was the home of the Miyazaki's about whom I have already written. Nearby, and on one evening I well remember, I recognised a young working girl from the office who was sitting outside her home with her mother. She gave me a nod and a wave, accompanied by a silly girlish giggle. It all seemed so natural.

Beyond the bridge

Once you were over the bridge you could walk along the embankment and follow the river towards the sea; or, turning to the left on the other side, you could go to Main street and the, shopping areas and the Aburaya ryokan (Japanese hotel) where, in the daytime, I sometimes had meetings with local officials. Straight ahead, you could walk into suburbia and wander between endless lines of houses. I knew that "my city beyond the bridge" was not heaven or paradise, and that it was not even today's modern city, but it was foreign. It was eastern and it was there to see. Was this just because of the glamour of the East as opposed to the West? No, I think not. It was a city with virtues and vices, joys and sorrows like any other community. Of sorrows, it had certainly had its share, but it was different because it was far removed from the towns and cities which I knew in distant Britain, and also because different peoples and their customs are always full of interest. As I moved on I knew that, before long, especially at night, I would be accosted. The usual approach to us was "Any sweets Ofsa San?", or the whistling of a black market ditty to a tune I have forgotten, which was a kind of password to rather dubious dealings. Little boys would be offering for sale their black market wares, while touts and others had less palatable wares to sell. Outwardly at least, neither approvingly nor disapprovingly, I silently ignored their offerings. Argument and curiosity would have been fruitless, and maybe dangerous. I remembered with a touch of shame, not so many months before as a young subaltern in Bombay, I had run hurriedly back to camp, rather than face a few harmless solicitations. I was now content to be sensible of the prevailing conditions, and not to be under any fanciful delusion as regards the Japanese character, or indeed human nature as a whole. What lay before me now was the logical outcome of a lost war, starvation, suffering, the emptiness of defeat, the shattering of long held beliefs, and an uncertainty of life and living. It was not just a study of Japan's present condition, painful and sad as that was. There was a lesson here which was of interest to everybody.

Main street, Aburaya hotel, and the shops

Entering Main Street, during the daytime in the early days, I would pass some general stores, which then alas, were not full of many wares. They hardly looked as if they were there for trade at all. Dirty windows, shabby fronts, and dusty boards seemed to say that like the country they were tired and nothing really mattered any more. A little further on, there were closed shops, and shops which were almost bare and un-inviting. Except for an odd notice about salt or some other product, I never knew what they were selling. But not by any means was everything always gloomy. There was a coffee shop and the still very stately Aburaya ryokan for officers. If ever you felt like a chat, Mama San and her twin sister who were the owners of the inn would always make you welcome. The Aburaya was indeed the perfect example of a fine Japanese inn. It was a several storied building which, with the help of time and creeper, looked beautiful, snug, and secluded. When, in the evening dusk, its lights flickered from its several balconies which overlooked the river and the sea, it was just like a haven of rest in the side of a beautiful mountain. Not very often now, however, did the two sisters throw open its large banqueting rooms, or let its comfortable rooms to residents. Hotels were suffering. Occasionally, I organised a small party or even a dance—sometimes legally, sometimes not,—and bringing this slight touch of business to them—I was always, Sumisu San. I would join them on their high stools at the back of their hotel in the cool of a summer's evening and feel the warmth of their greeting. When I left at the end of September it was "Why must you go, Sumisu San?—come back soon!" and, I was sure they meant every word. Not far from the Aburaya, there was a busy little centre of activity especially in and around the barbers; where time didn't seem to matter. In the barbers you could if you wished have a chat with the manager; he seemed to have very little else to do. If you were in a hurry you could shave yourself—no one really minded. I had had my own hair cut there on more than one occasion by some pretty young lady assistant which I must admit for me at that time was a totally novel experience. While I sat there silently having my hair cut, I remember once listening to some delightfully flirtatious chatter between an attendant and a customer. On another occasion, a bashful young policeman who, having presumably been waiting for attention, was standing and shaving himself,—although to be truthful, as I looked at his smooth, sallow, face, it didn't seem that there was anything there to shave at all. Towards the end of my stay in Japan, one of the stores near the Aburaya had become very enterprising and was very popular with the troops looking for souvenirs to take home. Among other little treasures which I bought was the work of a local artist which captured an invaluable memory of the Iwakuni area, a lovely painted scroll, then called a kakemono but now called a kakejuku, of two young kimono clad damsels walking along a narrow path beside a swiftly flowing Nishiki river. Between the path and the river, there are some small leafy bushes and also an impressively large tree whose branches are stretching out across the water towards the other side of the river. Teasingly, the branches are hiding from view parts of Iwakuni's famous Golden Bridge, the Kintai bashi. Adrift in the river, are two or three small rowing boats or little canoes; while, way in the background behind it all, there are the tall, towering, green hills completing the picture. When I arrived back in England I had the scroll mounted and famed, and it has proudly adorned the lounge in my home ever since.

Evening walks

My daytime walks were not as frequent as my evening strolls because in the daytime I was fully occupied at work. They were also very different. As an evening wears on, there is something frightening about walking through a sleeping city, hearing almost the heaves and sighs of sleep. One's own behaviour too seems a little improper. At the same time, however, perhaps I felt—a little super human perhaps—an accredited reviewer,—a cut above weary mortals who always have to take a daily quota of inactivity. Here was an opportunity to explore. As I walked through the streets, I was amazed at the number of homes which seemed to be on top of one another, but it would be wrong to say that there was any sense of disorder or chaos anywhere. Everywhere was crowded, but everything was tidy and had its carefully allotted place. It was only when, with unwarranted impertinence, I might occasionally catch a glance of a whole family packed together asleep in awkward positions beneath large mosquito nets that I realised the harsh conditions in which some families were living. Japan was baring her soul, but very stoically and bravely suffering the pain. It was not uncommon during those hot summer evenings to find a man seated with his family outside their home gazing at any passerby or staring blankly into space preferring the fresher and cooler conditions outside to perhaps a more unhealthy rest inside. Once in the company of a friend I came upon such a family, and after some cautious but unmistakable scrutiny as to who and what we were, we were offered room on their two benches. I sat between father and son on one bench. My friend sat between mother and daughter on the other. A cigarette for Papa, and sweets for Mama and the two children; and our friendship with all of them was assured. We were all ready for a chat.

A typically local discussion

We were told that we should have seen Japan when Papa (Takada San) was young. Life then was happy and prosperous. Japan was irresistible. There is nothing Japan would not have done for a visitor. Our countries had been allies. Takada San said that he was still the same Takada as he was then. Life was very pleasant, and the world was at peace. But, things went wrong at the top. With his memory stirred, Takada San became animated. The spirit of Japan, he said, still ran in the veins of the humblest peasant; but, of the future, and with a glance at his two children now playing in the roadside dirt, he said he was less sure. He did not regret his country's defeat and he did not fear unfair treatment from its conquerors. He did, however, fear this continual disturbance and instability in his life. It was already rumoured that the big powers could not agree, and why were there no Russian or Chinese armies of occupation here? What would Japan's position be if there was further conflict? The topic was becoming a little uncomfortable, so we abandoned it, and soon it was time to go. However, Mr Takada's views had left us with much room for thought. It had been a very pleasant encounter. We put on our peaked caps, which earlier we had taken off for comfort just after we arrived, and we trudged on somewhat regretfully into the enveloping darkness ahead. The children were shouting, "They were "afsers", daddy, "afsers", did you know?", and we looked back wistfully at their four dimly receding forms. We were in the midst of a modest and tiny fishing community

Chapter 18: Walkabouts in Iwakuni

at an unearthly hour of night, witnessing the simple ways of countless millions of people the world over, people who were entitled to their own views, as well as to a say in world affairs. Takada San had no immediate fears. What he did fear was the conduct and ultimate consequences of nations, and ruthless leaders all over the world, over whom he thought he had no influence. In perfect silence, and yet absolute harmony of mood, my friend and I continued our nocturnal wandering. This didn't seem like the Japan which had frightened the world. An odd light showed an aged widow working late with her sewing; another showed a factory watchman asleep at his post; and elsewhere, except for a group of employees at the railway station, was hushed in sleep. Back along the embankment, an old fisherman yawned and said a few words of greeting, as we walked passed him, with his boat tied to the shore in front of him. My friend and I had both been far too thirsty for knowledge to take heed of the clock or other worldly obstacles. Our thoughts ran deep at what we had seen and felt from our discussions; and, as if that was not enough, the comments and descriptions by my friend afterwards held me still for a while where I stood. His comments were so meaningful, delicate, and heartfelt, that they made me ask why he had never become an author. His reply, I thought, was typical of an Australian journalist. His only interest in writing he said was the thousand words a day which he had to write to earn his salary from his newspaper. My friend was of course the Australian wartime correspondent and room mate, Jack Evans, to whom I referred earlier. We continued to make similar walks in Iwakuni; and, on one occasion in broad daylight, we even walked in Hiroshima. The ground there had been cleared of its most dangerous debris, and new buildings were beginning to appear; but, conditions there were still very grim and forbidding. It was by no means an entertaining visit. Hiroshima's wounds were much harder to heal.

Chapter 19

The Iwakuni Cultural Society

Iwakuni Shin Bunka Domei

Very soon after I had arrived in Iwakuni, I had been told that there were several influential citizens in the city who wanted to form a society to discuss Japanese culture in its new environment. A few weeks before Jock's leaving us to go to Bofu, I was approached officially by the prospective organisers of such a society, the purpose of which was to study and discuss the different views, customs, and traditions of the Allies, and how these impacted on Japanese culture; and, if they were desirable, to decide how they could be integrated into Japanese society. The society had already given itself the rather pompous title of "Iwakuni Shin Bunka Doumei" or, literally, "The new Cultural Alliance of Iwakuni". The organisers wanted us not only to approve the formation of the society, but they also wished to extend its membership to the Allied Forces. Although, almost by instinct, I had doubts about the response of our Allied Forces to this invitation, it was I believed another welcome sign of how the Japanese people were responding to their misfortune. From the depths of depression, after the shocks and horror of Hiroshima and Nagasaki, they were now looking for ways to rise up and become a respected nation again. They were neither broken in spirit; nor had they given up the struggle

Chapter 19: The Iwakuni Cultural Society

to recover. As if by an irony of Fate, however, at the very time I was questioned, there was in my hands and on my desk, an outline of new rules as a first step in the Allied Forces' anti-fraternisation policy. Jock shook his head, and although he took the request to a higher level we had no doubt as to its initial refusal; which was of course the case. Our immediate reply was evasive, if not discourteous. We said that we did not know whether they could form such a society. This was a matter for the American Military Government. The American Liaison Officer, Mr Kawamura, would be able to advise them on that. Whatever the answer, however, there was no possibility of Allied Forces in Iwakuni being allowed to take part. The reason for this could be seen in the daily newspapers, and we quoted an extract from the Osaka Shinbun which stated that "Commonwealth troops would not be allowed to associate with the Japanese people, to enter their homes, or to take part in their family life, because of the many differences which existed between Japanese way of life and ours. Any misunderstanding, or breach of custom on our part, might be embarrassing and could hinder the smooth working of the Occupation". This was of course a very unsatisfactory reply. We did not imagine for a moment that members of the society at its inaugural meeting would be at all impressed; either by it, or by the behaviour of the very people whose manners and ideals they wanted to study.

Loopholes in the law

The very idea that we might embarrass the Japanese people was not of course accepted by either the organisers of the society, or by ourselves. It was moreover a severe blow to the Japanese people who, not unjustifiably, rated themselves as being one of the world's most hospitable people. As time progressed, however, we inevitably found that there ways we could overcome the stalemate. Due very much to the efforts of the Society and of our Security officer, Flt Lt. McLaughlin (Mark), whom I mentioned earlier, and with whom I had been in Burma many months before, and had also met again in Madras on my way to Japan, the authorities partly relented. A few selected British officers were allowed to attend meetings once per week in the capacity of lecturers. In my own case, the British Council in London had also expressed an interest in my meeting Japanese people with a view to letting them know more about the British way of life. At least for me this was step in the right direction. Mark was a young Scotsman, a graduate in the Classics, from the University of Glasgow. Mark's views and mine were of one accord and I lost no time in becoming an "attendant lecturer". I spent some excellent times with Mark in Japan, which I will refer to later; and he threw himself whole heartedly into what he regarded as his pet project. We spent many hours afterwards back in the UK reminiscing about those far off days. I was extremely fortunate that Mark of all people should have had this task allotted to him. His post as Security officer afforded him the opportunity to attend regular meetings of the society and, as his Number 2, I was very glad to go along and achieve my own aims. Mark in an official role was ensuring that there was no subversive activity in the Society; and I was promoting interest in the British way of life by comparing it with Japanese culture. Although Mark conformed to the very letter of the law on fraternisation and never breached it, he was always very sympathetic towards the citizens of Iwakuni. He listened patiently to their requests, and did whatever he could do for them within the law. The fact that Mark, did perhaps have stricter ideas about obeying the fraternisation laws than I did (especially about meeting families in the home), was a credit to his integrity. He really "showed the flag", and the Japanese people realised it. I particularly remember a long court case in which he had worked extremely hard, and had ultimately succeeded, in defending a young Japanese youth against a somewhat dubious charge. After that, Mark's reputation in the community was forever guaranteed.

<u>Principal members</u>

The principal members of the Society were all well respected citizens of Iwakuni. They included the local medical doctor (Dr Fujimura); the local dentist (Dr Ichioka); the school headmaster; and a business woman, who (like the Police chief's interpreter, Mickey) had spent a lot of time in America. In addition, I was extremely glad that one principal member of the Society was none other than Shizue, who with many thanks due to Jock, I had known almost from the minute I had arrived in Japan. Shizue was invaluable to me, especially as she was more than willing to help me prepare a couple of talks which I gave to the Society. A few notes on these two speeches, the first of which I gave on the evening of my first attendance at the Society, are given a little later. Nominally, Dr Fujimura was the Chairman of the Society. He was a very likeable personality, but he didn't seem to smile so much as the others and, behind his loose fitting spectacles and short trimmed moustache, I often had the feeling that he was worried about something. His hair was greying and, although still only middle aged and, although also he had unquestionable interest in the Society, he seemed to me to lack the energy and drive that the Society required. Under his guidance the Society managed to maintain the size of its membership but, even within the time of my association with it, its shape and character undoubtedly changed. Instead of audiences of a majority of keen spirited youths which we had at the beginning, they became meetings of a few studious youths, young girls in kimonos, and an increasing number of older persons. Rather than being an inspiration and guide for people, Dr Fujimura resembled more a man with a burden of his own. The local School headmaster, in whose premises we were always housed, was certainly a more prominent and active member of the Society. He looked distinguished in his dark coloured evening kimono or yukata. He introduced many sound arguments, but he was probably not capable of taking the Doctor's place or even becoming his faithful lieutenant. He was a little contemptuous of people whom he thought were bent on changing the Japanese culture he cherished. He refused in any way to put the blame for Japan's political failure, or the actions of its guilty war leaders, on to Japan's way of life and customs. I do not believe that was ever the intention of the Society but I suspected, at times, that he thought it was. It was noticeable that during lectures he always sat among the audience, and not at the top table. As for Shizue, she had changed a great deal during the two months since I used to visit her family with Jock. In her present setting she was much more confident and effective, if not the controlling force, behind the scenes. She dressed always, as if in defiance of Western custom, in a most immaculate kimono and had almost an air of superiority in her conduct. She did not make many suggestions of her own, but her translations from one language to another, and her explanations on others' behalf were brilliant. I could not help but be aware of something dynamic within her to which Japanese people now responded with sincere respect. It may have been her undoubted intelligence and talent which compelled this respect. It may have been that her family was able to help the Society socially or financially. It may even have been her new position with a Police detachment of the Allied Forces, which inspired fear in her audience; but, whatever it was, it was very noticeable. To be fair to Shizue, I don't think that she was ever aware of this effect which she had on people.

The committee and the top table.

The four most prominent members of the Society were Dr Fujimura, who was a well known local doctor; the Headmaster whom I had already met; the American style business woman; and Shizue, who was the chief interpreter. There was also a young secretary who took down copious notes at all meetings; but she took very little active part in the management of the Society's affairs. There were, on the other hand, usually four British officers at any meetings which I ever attended. These were Mark McLaughlin, an Education officer, me, and a Police Security officer, whose position at times seemed a little suspect. He joined in debates and in the responses to lectures; but his very presence, I thought, could only restrain free expression—especially of the younger and more keenly spirited men and women in whose ideas and ambitions I was interested in most of all. We four Westerners, together with the committee, and the industrious little secretary,—but with the exception of the headmaster who, as I have mentioned, would usually retreat into the audience,—always sat behind a long well polished table on which rested two or three bowls of flowers and stunted trees. Behind this profuse foliage, we could attempt as we pleased either to hide from, or show ourselves to, the audience in front of us. We four Europeans sat on Western style chairs while the others sat on wooden benches. The meetings were held in the main hall of the Iwakuni High School. It was a large and spacious room. This, however, together with its austere furniture arrangements, even on a warm summer's evening, chilled the atmosphere which, I often thought, ought to have been warmer and kindlier looking than it sometimes was. The first time I attended, I was introduced to the members of the society by Shizue; and I immediately felt myself at the nerve centre of hundreds of peering eyes, half of them friendly, some of them suspicious. Who was this new arrival? What was his function? Many knew that I was on the BCAIR headquarters staff and they were probably quite prepared to hold this against me. A whisper from Mark confirmed my impression. There were usually two speeches or lectures per meeting and, although I should have spoken first, I was allowed this time to follow the Education officer who spoke on a subject which was destined to become the substance of many more speeches and debates of the future.

The status of women

I sat patiently but anxiously through the Education officer's speech, which was translated brilliantly by Shizue, and was entitled the "Status of British women". Shizue was in excellent form as she pointed out the remarkable contrasts between English and Japanese womenfolk. I was overjoyed as I watched the tenseness grow. The men and boys in the audience began to fidget and look uncomfortable, but the girls leaned forward sometimes with elbows on their knees and beautiful faces of wonder lodged in their palms of their hands, as if they were in a marvellous world of dreams and seeing daylight for the very first time. A woman in England had the same rights as a man. She was barred from no profession. She could not be divorced without either her consent, or proof of her own misconduct. Her position could be higher than her husband's; and, what might seem unfair,—no lower. The future monarch in England would be a woman, and so on. Examples of what may have seemed like English ladies' tyranny over "poor men" seemed to be pouring out in an endless stream. The men in the audience stirred and were no doubt thinking, "What fools!". The girls, with their tongues in their cheeks, were enjoying themselves. Even Dr Fujimura forced a smile of approval, as he pushed his spectacles back to the bridge of his nose from which they had slipped; but no one in the Society really believed us. Our very attitude, it was thought showed that deep down we too belied in the inferiority of women. So incredulous was the audience that at Question time we were almost cross examined. Why? Why? Why? Why did Englishmen stand up in trains to let women sit down? Was it pity for their humble status, or their humble station and physical weakness? Or, was it our heritage from mediaeval times; when, on our own admittance, women did have fewer rights than men? Our attempts to define chivalry and gallantry towards women were met with polite silence but with a complete failure to understand. To the Japanese mind, equality was to be found more in allowing, or indeed forcing, women to work hard in the paddy fields, or in factories. At nine o'clock questions relating to the Education officer's speech were brought to a halt. The Society respectfully concluded that what we believed in was not really equality of the sexes,—that could never be. What we were talking about was a very inestimable quality of bestowing kindness! I was a little disappointed that we had not made more of an impression.

British Youth

As soon as the Education officer had finished his speech, Dr Fujimura welcomed me to the Society and introduced me to the audience. He said that I had been given a free hand in choosing my subject and that I had chosen to give a talk about the role and activities at the present time of young people in Great Britain. I was then formally invited to sit in the chair invariably occupied by the speaker. As I began to speak, the secretary picked up her pad and pencil and I imagined her as the devil's angel about to take a summary of evidence before admitting me to hell. For some unknown reason I was just very nervous. The doctor, my usually very friendly Shizue, and everyone, seemed to become potentially hostile, as they waited. Even the headmaster, who was now back in the audience, crossed his legs, drew in the folds of his sombre kimono, narrowed his lips, and made a wry smile which spread grimly over his dark but shaven face. It was all very frightening. But then, I noticed a sudden twitch in the headmaster's lips as my eyes challenged his—and I saw that there was also a reassuring twinkle in his eye. I knew at that moment that it was confirmation of our continuing friendship. It was very timely and welcome; and it gave me instant relief. I made my speech, and Shizue translated it piece by piece impeccably. The whole talk, interspersed with translation, took no more than half an hour. There was a short hush, some moderate applause, and then a sudden noise like a bursting bubble. I had, it seemed, won the confidence of the audience; and, as a reward, I was being deluged by a barrage of questions. Everyone wanted to ask a question which Shizue translated and answered magnificently, even permitting me occasionally to speak in Japanese. I did, after all have a complete copy of Shizue's translation. In my reference to the independence, and sometimes the pranks which English girls get up to, I kindled the interest of all the girls in the audience. Many of them forgot that there were men in the audience, to whom according to their customs they might perhaps have showed more deference, but they leaped up and shouted; and did everything they could, except sing, to attract my attention.

Question time

It was not a very good speech, but it was my first; and if I did not convince everyone about the soundness of Western ideas, I had at least convinced them of my sincerity. Whatever fear members may have had of me,—secret agent, security officer, policeman, or whatever role they had attributed to me, I was now a member of the Society. I was one of them. The change from that moment on was gratifying, and forever after I cherished my connection with the Society and my indebtedness to Mark for making it possible. By far, most of the questions which followed my talk were in response to what I had said about the Boy Scouts and Girl Guides. There was a surprisingly persistent interest in these movements and in the good which they do. I quickly disillusioned any questioner who thought that the movements had anything to do with the preparation for war. The Government had no control or connection with these movements whatsoever. They were entirely independent. There was in fact similar but smaller organisation in England called the Boys Brigade of which my brother had been a member. It too was completely independent. The Boy Scouts itself had started in Great Britain by Lord Baden Powell in the early 1900's. His initials, BP adopted to mean "Be Prepared" had become the proud motto of all Boy Scouts and Girl Guides all over the world. The boys and girls were taught how to do things, develop skills, how look after others, and how to fend for themselves in all kinds of situations. Much of the audience's interest in the Boy Scouts probably stemmed from comparisons with the chivalrous days of Japan's illustrious Samurai who also had their own code of honour, loyalty, and constant desire to do good things. There were striking similarities. There were also questions as to how far this youthful independence, free thought, individuality, inquisitiveness, and thinking for oneself, which I had stressed, extended into schools, the home, and society generally. The answers I gave revolved round the importance of self discipline, self responsibility, and consideration for others, each of which had to be taught alongside all the other activities in which young people were being encouraged to take part. The barrage of questions continued unabated until about 10.30, when we adjourned. The topic had been purely about the youth of present day Britain. I could have gone on all night, but our excitement and fervent interest was racing with the clock. A rather conspicuous time check by the British Police officer present signalled that our time was up. Dr Fujimura wound up the evening beautifully thanking me from the depth of members' hearts and he hoped that I would make further speeches to them quite frequently in the future. A lady member from the audience presented me with a lovely bouquet of flowers, and the headmaster asked me if I would kindly give a similar talk to his teaching staff. I was over the moon and my character had never been more in danger of self false pride. We four British officers returned to our Mess for good night drink. Spurred on by the evening I had just experienced, I was determined to help the Society all I could. I knew I could depend on Emiko and the Miyazaki's to help me understand the Japanese peoples' point of view, and that I could count no less on Shizue to produce a perfect translation of my views—in faultlessly written characters, and also nicely bound, like the one she had given me for this one. Some accounts of further meetings which I attended at the society are given a little later. This was I felt a good way for me to help create "Peace in Our time!".

Chapter 20

Contact with the Miyazaki's is Resumed

Effect of Jock's departure

Jock's departure from Iwakuni, when he rejoined his unit in Bofu, was a sad loss to me in many ways, but especially because it had broken my contact with the Miyazaki's. Emiko had left our camp, as I knew she would; and there seemed no way, I could arrange to see her. In the day time, it didn't matter. I was fortunate that I had so many things to occupy my time. These helped me not to pine for Jock, his inimitable presence, and all his valuable social contacts. I still had my vastly interesting work in the office, difficult problems to solve, the continuing build up of our forces, demands to find room for our new arrivals, and a variety of time consuming visits to our headquarters of many important personalities. This is to say nothing of requests for information, especially in the early days, by AVM Bouchier and the Air Officer Administration, which always demanded my immediate attention. I was always extremely eager to provide them smartly and very promptly with the information which they asked me for, and particularly on local matters with which I always felt so au fait. Socially, too, as I have indicated, I had joined the Iwakuni Cultural Society. However, in the evenings, when I had used to do so many things with Jock, it now seemed longer than ever to bedtime. Dinner in the Mess was at six o'clock, and there was a light supper about nine o'clock. Time began to drag. That was never a problem when Jock was there. But now, my thoughts would stray back to that wonderful first evening with Emiko and her family. I could not persuade myself to call on the Miyazaki's; and, the anti fraternisation laws were also beginning to bite. Given time, I might have done it but for the first week or so I could only imagine my own effrontery and impudence at presenting myself at their door. It seemed I had been given a glimpse of what I really craved for, only to see it all suddenly snatched away—almost as a punishment for asking for too much. There seemed no way out. The Miyazaki's were a long way away from me now. Emiko it seemed had walked out of my life. I was back to evenings in the Mess.

The wanderer returns

Then, suddenly out of the gloom, not long afterwards, the wanderer returned. Jock came through on a flying visit, and being free that evening, suggested that we dropped in on the Miyazaki's. As soon as I saw him in the Mess, my face brightened and my heart missed a beat. I knew what we would surely do. It was great to see him, but it was even greater when he suggested we should pay Emiko a visit. He was surprised I had not been there without him. He assured me that I would have been very welcome; but he nodded understandingly "Oh, you English", he said. I couldn't get there quick enough; and we had to walk there too. We couldn't risk taking a jeep now, and then leaving it parked outside the Miyazaki's; even if we could have secured one. Jock wanted to show me some photos and pictures of Japan, many of which I had seen before. "Oh come on, Jock" I said "we really haven't got much time". It was nearly nine o'clock when we arrived and from that moment I knew that my future friendship was firmly established. I wasn't awkward this time. I was out to please and at my best. Our hosts were eager to see us and asked why I had never called. They wanted to know too how Jock was faring in Bofu. They said how much they had missed him and looked forward to further occasional visits. We had not been expected, but our welcome was as great as ever. We were led into their best room, although later in the summer, I was welcomed into another room which I even preferred. In came tea, and a few eatables, and we all sat down and talked over the hibachi. Food was far from plentiful in Japan but the Miyazaki's had delved once again into their small supply. We remonstrated, in as friendly way that we could but they refused to listen, and insisted on our eating. It was easy to see how hurt they would have been had we persisted. I can see Jock's face even now as he tackled the "o mocha" or rice cakes, but my disappointment too was to follow. It was his turn to laugh and I discerned an inward chuckle. We did our best with them but I didn't think we would ever be likely to say we enjoyed them. We carried on eating successfully until a much more interesting course arrived. For the Western palate, regrettably, "o mocha" seemed far too stodgy. But, Jock and I would be the last people in Iwakuni to complain, especially in the face of such kindness, and self sacrifice of their own precious food. We never referred to our feelings on the matter again and it was closed.

Animated chatter

Our conversation was bright and light, and it skipped quickly from one subject to another,—Jock's hometown, his extensive farm there, comparisons between Australian and Japanese agriculture, his family, my family, Emiko's birthplace in Hawaii, the price of rice and a packet of cigarettes both now and before World War 1, as well all manner of little items which talked about help to make the world go round. Jock was never short of a topic. If interest should flag he could save any conversation; he could indeed save any situation. We spoke mainly in English except for my interjection in Japanese if I thought there was any chance of a misunderstanding, not that I probably elucidated anything; although possibly, in the end, my translation did lead to a less incorrect understanding. I suspected that Mrs Miyazaki's knowledge of English was even better than Emiko's; but, if it was, she always concealed this. Mrs Miyazaki never attempted to correct Emiko, or to take Emiko's place as the prime talker on behalf of the Japanese speaking company. It was the kind of affection between mother and daughter which greatly impressed me. It was also contrary to my earlier belief that Japanese daughters had no place at home, except an inferior one. I was at the time preparing to give a talk to the Cultural Society comparing the status of women in Britain with that of Japanese women, believing that Japanese women were far more submissive. Now that I had seen many Japanese women in very expensive clothes and little girls in darling, petite, and highly colourful kimonos, which were certainly not cheap to buy or to make, it was perhaps time for me to reconsider my ideas. I was now seeing Japanese home life at closer quarters. Mrs Miyazaki wielded a lot of power. She affected her husband's decisions, and she was just as capable of reprimanding her son as she was of reprimanding her daughter. Her love for her children was equally divided. Emiko, on her part, voiced her opinions just as much to the annoyance of her younger brother as my sister used to bother me. This tale of feminine inferiority was at least exaggerated if it was not entirely untrue. I felt I wanted to tell the world. I had been told, rightly or wrongly, that; according to the law of Buddha, women's only hope for salvation was always to be good and obedient to men, so that women might then become men in their next life. Only by doing this could they reach Nirvana, the Buddhist heaven. I looked round at faces in the Miyazaki home. I didn't believe that anyone believed it, or even wanted to believe it.

One of the family

It seemed to me, sitting there among such warm friends, in a foreign country, sharing their intimacy, in their most cherished sanctuary, that I was truly in heaven. Certainly for me in Japan at that time, after the cheerless, comfort of our camp, night after night, there was no nearer place to heaven than the Miyazaki's home. My visits to them from then on became more and more frequent and I found myself becoming a little too dependent on them for my out of camp education. I was visiting them about three evenings a week. Even to me, it seemed hardly fair that I should expect one family to provide me with the amusement and interest which was lacking elsewhere. But I could not stop myself from going there; and, greedily, accepting their hospitality. On the other hand, I did feel I was becoming more and more one of the family and I felt this especially on one Sunday evening. I called on the family about my usual time which then was about half past seven o'clock. I had given no prior warning or intimation of my going there. I had been given a standing invitation to go there, as and when I wanted, and this was one of my responses. For once, however, the family didn't expect me and was entertaining guests. I realised how inconsiderate it was of me, and I wanted to beat a hasty retreat. But, Mrs Miyazaki would have none of it. She ushered me into my favourite room amidst a large circle of people. I was introduced and announced to the fold as

Chapter 20: Contact with the Miyazaki's is Resumed

a mother might introduce her son, warmly, but almost reprovingly, for being late. Almost by telepathic communication I knew I was expected to be on my best behaviour and to sit as the guests were seated on cushions in the Japanese way. I knelt down with both knees together and, with my body upright, and sitting on the back of my outstretched heels, I swung both hands forward to rest them open palmed over my two knee caps. Mrs Miyazaki was pleased to see me as such an obedient "son". She betrayed a faint smile because, as I assumed she thought, my sitting there like must have been rather painful for me. She nodded approvingly. I don't think I ever liked her more than I did at that very precise moment.

Conversation at dinner

A place was set for me and I joined in the general drift of conversation. There were four guests, all of them relations. There were two men, a lady with much spirited energy who guided most of the chatter, and a small, pretty, young girl of about thirteen years of age who was Emiko's cousin. No special limelight was thrown on me, however, and for that I was grateful. It was generous of them to look at me as one of them and not as a foreigner. When the meal was over, Mrs Miyazaki was visibly relaxed. Just as if she had told me with her own lips, I gathered from here that I could now sit at ease and cross my legs. Men were allowed to sit cross legged, but the ladies, poor dears, always had to sit upright. I felt a satisfying delight in obeying instructions, accepting my new status as a member of the family, and taking part in such obviously Japanese customs. The guests lived in Hiroshima and had survived the atom bomb, although much of their property had been lost. Nearly two hundred thousand people had perished in their hometown. They had seen horrid scenes, arms and legs scattered over devastated land. They had lost friends and watched others maimed and crippled so much, that they even felt guilty that they had survived when they compared their own good fortune the terrible suffering of others. Yet, for all this they remained friendly to me and to the world outside. They showed no sign of bitterness or hatred. It was wonderful to witness this perfect example of "love your enemy". Like many of my own folk at home, they had lost much; but, still their eyes, their gestures, and very expressions all seemed to implore, "let us all forget, and begin again,—as friends". In my own thoughts, I was thinking, but

I didn't say, what a pity it is that our Occupation policy doesn't lets us foster these feelings. How unfavourably did our recently announced fraternisation policy contrast with these friendly signs of real human nature? What injustice were we inflicting on our former enemies?

A little introspection

As cold weather gave way to warm, grey skies turned to blue, and the evening insects became noisier, such thoughts as these came to me more frequently. Muddy paddy fields became luxuriously rich and green, like beds of the purest silk, and cherry blossoms had bloomed, faded, and then fell. I was impressed by nature's changing face no less in Japan as elsewhere. But, while Nature was moving on, it often seemed, with the anti fraternisation policy again, that human relations between nations, between the Occupiers and the Occupied, were not really moving at all. Like many youths of my age at the time I had lofty ideals; but, there were so many obstacles to achieving them, I felt helpless in not being able to do anything about it. At times I must have felt depressed, seemingly locked in a prison without bars, and subjected to mental torture. Opportunities seemed to be disappearing with each movement of the fingers on the clock; opportunities which might never occur again; opportunities which would promote permanent goodwill between all people. Others might have a chance e to do better than me later, but why shouldn't I be given a chance too? To my hosts, the Miyazaki's, I probably even appeared quite melancholy about it, but fortunately they often supplied me with the welcome mental comfort I needed. "Genki o dase" or "Cheer up!" they would say. And then follow this with a little general explanation of their philosophy of life. This would bring me to my senses, and who indeed could have done so better than my hosts with such sweet cajoling in such sweet surrounds? After five minutes in their home, I would brace myself and describe and tackle, as far as my limited Japanese vocabulary would permit, many of the huge and disturbing world problems with which we were beset. Looking back now, I can see that the Miyazaki's realised my mental state. Just as Emiko was treated for her weaknesses, although they were few, so I was humoured for mine. In other words, I was one of them and I loved them for it.

Chapter 20: Contact with the Miyazaki's is Resumed

Introducing Peter

Partly to obviate suspicion on myself for my nocturnal visits, and because he was also genuinely interested, I introduced a friend to the Miyazaki's; and together we visited Emiko in her home on many occasions. Peter, for that was his name, was extremely grateful for the introduction and never hesitated to ask me to go with him. Later, I believe he also used to call on her alone, when I was busy at work. The Miyazaki's welcomed him and feted him as they had done me. Had I any streak of jealousy in me it would have emerged then, because Peter was not only good looking and handsome, with qualities which I lacked, but he was very easy in conversation, and less restrained than I was. He appealed on sight to the Miyazaki's. Temporarily for the moment at least, I was No.2. Had it been a fight for romance at this time I would have lost hands down. Peter with his good looks, his curly hair, his smooth forehead, his broken Japanese and Pidgin English, his row of medals and his wings (for he was a pilot) would have made him an irresistible competitor. Indeed when Emiko gave him a photograph of herself, before she gave one to me, I felt a little hurt, although it was only proper that he should have it because he was leaving Japan long before I did. Of course, very few of our colleagues would probably have believed us. No story in fiction would permit such a friendship as ours without a resort to romance. And yet, in truth, we maintained together, and I continued afterwards, a faithful and perfectly innocent friendship with a Japanese family which, as far as I was concerned, had a daughter who was the prettiest girl in Japan. There was nothing at the Miyazaki's that we couldn't do together; and, Peter and I became staunch friends cementing a cheerful companionship which could not have been bettered. This was a little band of friendship in a corner of desolate Japan which gave us all hope for the future.

Chapter 21

Visit to the Local Mrs Vanderbilt and My First Tea Ceremony

<u>Invitation impossible to refuse</u>

The deep significance of O Cha-no-yu, the Japanese Tea ceremony and its influence on Japanese history and culture, was widely known and had been discussed at an early meeting of the Cultural society. I was also aware of its importance from my study of the Japanese language. I had read about the remarkable tea ceremony stories which have been told about the 16th century tea master Sen-no-Rikyu; and his famous follower, Lord and General, Hideyoshi. By still revering their own ancient and traditional customs like the Tea ceremony, the Japanese people were I believe helping themselves, not only to recover from their feelings of utter devastation which they had recently experienced, but also to return to normal life and living. I had however never witnessed a live performance of the ceremony, let alone taken part in one. This sad omission in my experience was about to be suddenly corrected. It came about by the connivance of Chiefy's main interpreter, Mickey, and a graduate friend of hers who was a photographer at our headquarters. They both knew a very wealthy local lady named Mrs Fujimoto whom, Mickey proudly

Chapter 21: Visit to the Local Mrs Vanderbilt and My First Tea Ceremony

called, "the local Mrs Vanderbilt", the name of a well known wealthy American lady. Mrs Fujimoto, who was renowned in Iwakuni for her wonderful tea ceremonies, had, during recent discussions with Mickey and the photographer, kindly invited Mark, two Press friends, and me, to one of her forthcoming ceremonies. I did not normally forgo such splendid opportunities; but, because of the possible grandeur of the occasion, the attendance of local men from the Press, and because of other rumours, I was more hesitant than usual. I certainly did not want openly to flaunt my disregard of our Force's anti fraternisation policy, or to dispel the confidence which the Service had in my attitude and demeanour. It was only after an assurance that nothing would be made public that I was persuaded to go. It was also reassuring to know that Mark, who was from the Security branch itself, would be going; since he presumably had some kind of clearance.

A remarkable and gracious lady

Mrs Fujimoto or Mrs Vanderbilt, as Mickey always insisted on calling her, was a very dear old lady, charming, cultured and immaculate,— an heroic and graceful figure, who after surviving violent changes in her former high ranking social life, was still as delightful, dignified, erect, and charming a person, as ever she was. For me, Mrs Fujimoto's name will always be associated with my idea of Japan's fascinating o cha-no-yu, not only because it was she who had made it possible for me to take part in two delightful performances of it, but also because her o cha-no-yu had all the traditional colour and regalia of the ceremony which has been performed in Japan throughout the ages. The performances were captivating. But apart from this invaluable service for me, Mrs Fujimoto herself was such a wonderful personality and real life character. At the Miyazaki's, I found the charm and hospitality of a happy warm hearted family despite really hard times. At the Namiwaki's, I had witnessed their touching attempts to find happiness at a time of personal bereavement, and in very reduced in circumstances, even if the latter were only temporary. Both families were typical of struggling family life throughout Japan immediately after the war. But, In Mrs Fujimoto, there was something different again. She was a gentle old lady, on her own; and, for her, there was only the past. For her, everything was still as it always had been. She persuaded herself that this was so; and also, at least temporarily, others like me, whenever she had a chance to show her skills. The meticulous length, to which she went to put on the tea ceremony, and her indifference to the disquiet of the world outside, had the effect of transporting people magically through the pages of time. For Mrs Fujimoto, the tea ceremony was more than a ceremony; it was a solemn observance and appreciation of life. She had abandoned what was, I had been told, an almost palatial residence, in order to live in the very house she had built for her tea ceremonies. She could truly be said to have dedicated the remaining years of her life to a belief in its cause. If we had ever wanted a faithful representation of the tea ceremony, we could not have found a better one anywhere than that of Mrs Fujimoto's, which was here on our doorstep.

Mrs Fujimoto's home

Mrs Fujimoto's home in Iwakuni's High street, into which Mark, I, and two Press friends were invited, had often intrigued me. Its doorway and its surrounding wooden framework were, I suppose, no different from those of many other Japanese homes. The stout wooden gate and the traditionally triangular covering to it which formed the entrance were common enough. But, Mrs Fujimoto's home had an air of mystery about it because of the high fences beyond the gate. Whatever could lie behind such high fences? I always had a feeling that one day I was destined to discover; and, now thanks to Mickey's perseverance, this was about to happen. To have entered the building openly with a clear conscience would have completed our happiness. But in the circumstances, neither the busy street nor the broad daylight around us permitted this. As it was, our attention was alert, and our minds were uneasy. Far from being a triumphal entry, it seemed a rather furtive, stealthy, and almost a shameful arrival. The alternative was out of the question. To have been watched by the public, the Police, or the Press, or even for the event to have been openly reported, would not only have incurred the Occupation forces displeasure and our discomfort, but it might also have brought much harm on our host and her property. In no time at all, Mrs Fujimoto's home might have been blacklisted and a sign erected outside, "Out of Bounds to all Allied troops". That must not happen! It was our duty to prevent it. Hence we made our undignified approach, a quick dash

Chapter 21: Visit to the Local Mrs Vanderbilt and My First Tea Ceremony

through the open gate, and through the fences, until we were safely on the other side and safely separated from public view.

Relaxation

At last we could relax. Suddenly there was no distraction, nothing but a wonderful experience, for us to savour and enjoy. We were wrapped in awe and wonder, as we stood still at the scene before us. It had a rare and delicate beauty. We were in a very beautiful miniature landscape garden, looking towards an attractive little building of very attractive but simple architecture which seemed to be calling us to enter. And yet, at the same time there was something less tangible, something magnetic and irresistible which drew us on, perhaps more in spirit than in body, towards its precincts. Quietly and gracefully, a gentle figure, dressed in a simple black robe, the author of it all, emerged from the house to greet us. The spell was complete. Our heartbeats changed their rhythm, and we ran forward to meet her. Mrs Fujimoto kneeled, bowed, and smiled; and with that, we knew that we were honoured guests. As we crossed the threshold of the house, a bell sounded announcing our arrival. Each stroke of the bell indicated a different guest. We entered and left the vestibule, following the directions of a young photographer who had been appointed as our guide and Master of Ceremonies. He led us into quite a large, cool, refreshing, room, which was strewn with gaily coloured straw curtains and which now looked out over a lovely sunlit garden. Everywhere was peace and tranquillity. There was very little furniture in the room, just a round beautifully polished table, a vase of carefully arranged flowers in the toko-no-ma, a few cushions on the floor, and also some canvas backed rests which looked rather like Western chairs with their legs sawn off. One's weight on the seat of the rests was strong enough to let us sit and lean back in safety. We had a feeling not only of sitting in a chair but also of squatting on the floor at, one and the same time.

Preliminaries

The room we were in appeared to be a room in which guests waited until the ceremony was about to begin. Ordinary refreshments not connected with the ceremony were served, introductions were made, and greetings exchanged as they could have been in any large drawing room in Europe. But our purpose was not just to enjoy the afternoon.

It was to take in the full meaning of an ancient Japanese custom and to conjecture, at each successive stage, what was coming next. The company, we could already see, was larger than we had expected. Dr Fujimura and a friend from the Iwakuni Cultural society had already arrived, and; through partly drawn curtains, we could see a little way into the area in which we imagined the main part of the ceremony would take place. Behind the curtains, we could see several young ladies in kimonos preparing things, and occasionally peeping through the curtains to see who we were. Our guide explained that the girls were simply eager to see the foreigners and guests to whom they would shortly be displaying their talents. Mrs Fujimoto explained that instead of officiating, she would also be a guest while one of the girls would act as hostess; another girl, since we had declined the offer, would act as chief guest. All the girls, she said, had studied the tea ceremony since childhood; and they were expected to give as good a performance as might be witnessed anywhere. Whatever fears we had had of monotony from a long ceremony were instantly dispelled by the colour and charm of these, cultured, and well bread young ladies raring to perform. There was no end to the happiness which was waiting for us.

Purification

Our guide whom we now called Fuji San, with no other justification than the fact that he knew Mrs Fujimoto, provided us with garden slippers and led us along a narrow winding path between rockery, flowers, trees, and stonework, away from the house towards a quiet sequestered spot in the garden where we were asked to undergo the formality of Purification. This we did by rinsing our hands and mouth at a small basin prescribed by custom. This was to show our willingness to worship purity as a token of respect to our host, before re-entering the house. At this point, our head guest, after seeing that we were all "purified", led the way through a small rectangular hatch into the house. One of our colleagues was, somewhat, a little large in size; and had some difficulty in navigating the hatch. He only succeeded after being pushed hard from behind. The purpose of such a small entrance and low doorway is intended to arouse in guests a feeling of humility, thankfulness, and respect. It is an ingenious way of displaying these qualities. Either one bowed and bended; or, one stayed outside.

Chapter 21: Visit to the Local Mrs Vanderbilt and My First Tea Ceremony

Fuji San had disappeared for a moment, while inside, Mrs Fujimoto and the deputy host were now waiting to receive us. There was no hurry. Fujimoto San spoke in Japanese in order to retain a genuine atmosphere of solemnity, and she gave us a general outline of the Tea ceremony's purpose. She supposed that we had learned about it from the Cultural Society. She hoped we were enjoying it and said she would gladly attempt to answer any questions. I was still in my dream world. There had been no need for Fuji San to ask us to sever all our worldly connections. I had done that the moment I had left the High street. Mrs Fujimoto and the deputy host then led us on, as we moved in perfect serenity. It was as if life itself had been hushed. Firstly, we entered a small room made entirely of bamboo, beautifully polished and clean, and we then went into a larger room of pure pine, each with enough simple beauty to strike chords of joy into the hearts of the hardest. This was perfect peace; inducing in us, not rest or laziness, but new mental agility and inspiration. Between these walls of different woods, there was sheer purity; no problem was too difficult; no mystery too deep to ponder. I would have stayed but, as if by magic, we found ourselves back in the large reception room where we had started; and where we had earlier espied the young, lively, kimono clad girls peeping at us through the curtains.

Taking our seats

Each of us was now allotted a place in the room of the ceremony. The girl as head guest took her cushion, which was to be her seat, next to the veranda curtain and nearest to the toko-no-ma. I was next, followed by other girls, colleagues, Dr Fujimura and friend, and Mrs Fujimoto, in that order, filling three sides of the room. The hostess, deputising for Mrs Fujimoto, sat squarely in front of the toko-no-ma facing the guests. By her side, there was a brazier, a kettle, and other utensils, for making tea. But, before we took up formal sitting postures which were required of us, or indeed before we had really sat down at all, there was a period of paying compliments which lasted on and off throughout the ceremony. Dr Fujimura went down on his knees as if he were about to pray and stayed there for about five minutes. He admired the fine arrangement of flowers which decorated the toko-no-ma. Others guests also, including Mark and I, who had recently been instructed in the art of Ikebana, or flower arrangement, made similar compliments. Our two Press friends, who were perhaps a little suspicious of the sincerity of all of this, sat still and took no part in the ritual. They did however atone for their solecisms;—by taking a massive number of photos and by drawing an amazing number of sketches of the proceedings. Mrs Fujimoto showed her gratitude to all these compliments, by instantly making further invitations to her" humble home", and by the rush of colour which suddenly lit up her normally pale wan face.

Tea Ceremony Par Excellence

At last we reached the Tea Ceremony itself. Tea was finally made, and each minute step in its making was a dedicated, perfected, delicate, solemn, and finely measured operation. No soldier would have drilled with more precision than that which our hostess displayed, both in making and serving the tea. The samurais of old Japan had embraced it in exactly the same way. It was not an unmanly custom. However, whereas the timing, and the exactness required of a soldier is because of the discipline of his calling, it seemed to me that the motivation here of our host and her guests that afternoon, was religious. Our hostess and guests were at prayer. Mrs Fujimoto may have derived both pride and pleasure in having such a time honoured ceremony performed so accurately and beautifully; but the meticulous inspection of the utensils, kettle, bowl whisk, and spoon, and the exquisite care with which we all treated them, no matter how old, worn, or inexpensive they were, was nothing else but worship,—silent worship,—to the God of Utility. Although she did not speak; she was saying to all of us that all things in this fleeting world of ours have value. Every single article, whether common and cheap to buy or not, has its use; and, in its use, it has beauty. This reverence for utility was a belief held not only by Mrs Fujimoto and those present but also widely throughout Japan. It possibly has relevance to the ingenuity which the Japanese people showed, at that time, in finding purpose in useless things, in making new things out of old, and often in making much from hardly anything. By clinging to these long held beliefs it was also helping the Japanese people recover from their present feeling of desolation and isolation after the war. We guests played our part as well as we could. Like everyone else, we examined meticulously, the tea bowl before we drank from it, appreciating the way it was made, its size,

Chapter 21: Visit to the Local Mrs Vanderbilt and My First Tea Ceremony

shape, and quality, looking at it from all angles, and at the same time glancing at our hostess and paying her our silent but very meaningful compliments. We felt that we were co-operating in a true and genuine Japanese Tea ceremony, which was faithful in every way to the established tradition.

End of a memorable day

Hereon, again thinking of us, the performance was possibly curtailed a little. Mrs Fujimoto even apologised for being unable, due to outside conditions, to provide us with more suitable fare. This only made us appreciate even more the lengths to which she had gone to entertain us, and at the same time had educated us in the true meaning of the ceremony. It had been a remarkable achievement. We then withdrew from the scene of the ceremony and moved back into the waiting room where we had started. Almost instantly, there began a veritable babble of conversation among us. Impressions were exchanged, questions were asked, and then, even at this late stage, we were introduced one by one to all the young girls who had so charmingly played their parts in the ceremony. Mark and his two Press colleagues, and I, were continuously asked for our views of the Tea ceremony and its place in Japanese history, whether we thought it was a good thing or otherwise. The Press, naturally were anxious to get people to pose for camera and crayon. Mrs Fujimoto, not to be outdone, asked us all to go into the garden to have a group photograph taken of the whole company. It had all been arranged. A photographer professional was waiting to receive us. No wonder he smiled at his easy task. What a happy group of people we must have seemed, as the lovely afternoon sun lit up the whole colourful scene. Gay kimonos, happy smiling faces, a beautiful garden before us, and a heavenly fairy tale home beside us. It was right and proper that such happiness was recorded. Mrs Fujimoto had good reason to be happy. She had brought together a group of like minded people for a most enjoyable afternoon. These included Dr Fujimura, representing the Cultural society; Fuji San, an excellent guide; and some really talented young girls, allowing them to display their skills in performing the rigours of the tea ceremony so meaningfully. Not least, it had given some lovely young damsels a perfect excuse to wear their priceless kimonos probably for the first time in years. Mark and I—in a way—were British ambassadors at a

Japanese national custom. For me, the ceremony was more than the perfect performance of a traditional art. It symbolised goodness in the devotees' character, a desire for tranquillity, and an appreciation of the good things in life. I like to associate Mrs Fujimoto in every way with this praiseworthy aspect of Japanese character. I went there again on many occasions. My respect for Mrs Fujimoto never wavered. She once showed me round parts of her home and the only room in the house with a lock on it, in which I gathered some pretty young maiden had once slept, but she would never expand on the story; and I was left just to wonder. She showed me the elaborate family shrine, and valuable pieces of china to which she still lovingly held on to. She would tell me over a cup of tea of her earlier life, not exciting as such, because girls in her day, she said, were not exciting; but, they did have passion. She had been devoted to a man she had loved passionately but that was now only in her memory. Her present circumstances, her earlier luxury, politics, war, or any regrets, if she did have them, she would never discuss; and I liked her all the more for it. Even on the morning I left Japan for home, I called in to see her. I wanted to recapture and relive again, for a moment, my first impressions, and love, of that lovely home and garden.

Chapter 22

The Cultural Society and Humour

Absence of humour in our lectures

As time rolled by, Mark and I became more and more engrossed in the work of the Cultural Society. We were particularly interested in members' reaction to speeches by Armed Forces personnel. Before preparing a speech, I would usually collect as many Japanese ideas on the subject I could. Emiko and her family were invaluable in giving me their views on a subject which enabled me to anticipate the types of question which we might get from the audience. After the event, Shizue would give me notes of the topics raised. These were always nicely and carefully written in Japanese characters, and I would often pass them on to other Japanese people, encouraging them to comment in their own language. However, in all our discussions there was usually one quality which seemed to be missing—and that was humour. Everything discussed seemed to be taken as if it was so dreadfully serious. Both Mark and I believed that humour was often very useful in resolving a dispute, or when trying to reconcile opposing views. A joke or a wisecrack was a good way of introducing a difficult subject. We called it "breaking the ice". Discourse would then often continue in a more friendly way. Whenever discussion became too serious, a playful joke, or an amusing reference, would often restore a cheerful atmosphere. However, we also realised that humour could sometimes go wrong. Some people might misunderstand it, and it might then have the opposite effect to what is intended. If this happened, we would say that some people had a different sense of humour. What one person thought funny was not necessarily funny to another. It was on one such evening, when we were pondering this problem, that Mark was induced to give a talk to the Society on humour. Unfortunately, we hadn't considered the dangers sufficiently. We learned them as a result of his talk.

Humour from Scotland

Mark began by noting that several of us in the society had frequently noted that some of the subtle points which we had made in our talks, to which we might have expected a smile or two, or a chuckle, or even a laugh, had merely often passed unnoticed. These were usually amusing anecdotes, silly situations we had been in, or perhaps some good humorous events which had happened probably at the speaker's expense, or at least where the speaker had not been seen in a very flattering position. We were puzzled at this and wondered afterwards if we had made a mistake in trying to evoke a smile at all, or whether our attempted witticisms were at least ill timed. It occurred to us after the talk that what makes Japanese people laugh might be very different from what evokes a laugh in us. Humour in Japanese eyes might be very different from our own; and, If this was so, it was probably worth investigating to see why this was so. It was certainly a difficult subject. Mark said afterwards that he rued the day he had ever decided to talk about it. In fact, he gave a very fine speech, which was well thought out and very well delivered. For us, it was very lively and entertaining. There were perhaps a few references to Scotland in the talk which, in Iwakuni, may not have been fully understood; but, I didn't think that this was sufficient to spoil the whole talk. Unfortunately after the talk, there was utter silence. The audience seemed stunned and remained deathly still. When we had laughed at Mark's "funny" stories, the audience had not seen anything funny in them at all, and probably thought we were crazy. No one in the audience asked a question of us. We had no alternative but to let the topic drop like a bad egg. The joke had been on us. Our conclusion from the evening was that; for humour to be effective in any country, it must at least have an interesting or amusing connection with something that is known about. The connection may be hidden, suspected or briefly known about, or it may be widely known about and obvious; but, if there is no known or suspected connection, the humour falls flat. In Mark's talk, any self deprecating remarks which implied, say, that Scotsmen were occasionally rather careful with their money, or that they were perhaps sometimes a little too fond of eating haggis, were probably completely unintelligible to the audience. His jokes had failed to raise even a smile.

Not all humour is amusing

It was a long time before the memory of Mark's talk receded from my mind. I knew that humour would not have helped us; for instance, when we were requisitioning citizens' property in the early days of the Occupation. That was far too serious a situation for making jokes. However, during the daily muster of manual labour, which we also discussed earlier, good humour did usually provide relief from a very unpleasant situation. The enforced work was then not half so bad or unbearable. We knew that Japanese people liked to laugh heartily, and to smile wryly, just as much as we did. It was obviously important to know when humour was likely to be effective or otherwise. The subject was worthy of further investigation; if not by the Society, then by us, individually. I decided that I would make a note of what I thought were humorous situations and discus these whenever possible with others. Most countries had words for joke, pun, and witticism, etc., but it was noticeable that there was no purely Japanese word for humour. In Japanese, the word for humour (humoa) had been borrowed from English. I often found it amusing to record some of the situations which I had found humorous, either because they seemed amusing to me at the time, but not necessarily so to my Japanese friends; or, because there were occasions when my friends had laughed and I did not.

Laughing at the loss of personal dignity

Some types of humour seemed to be common across the world, for example the occasional loss of personal dignity,—like slipping on a banana skin; provided, that is, that it is not physically harmful. In that case, it may too serious to be funny. In most countries, there is a tendency to find something amusing in the loss of dignity of local dignitaries—especially if they are inclined to be a little pompous in their manner. Slipping to the ground on a banana skin may be seen as someone getting their "come down", or their "come-uppance". It might be laughed at, and talked about, for many days afterwards. But, the victim doesn't necessarily have to be important to raise a laugh. I remember once, when Fusae San, my room girl, had laughed heartily for a full fifteen minutes, and just couldn't stop laughing, because a colleague of hers had slipped on a piece of slippery wet soap in the corridor outside my room. As she tried to explain to me, while still unable to control her laughter, her colleague had made a "shiri mochi" or, literally, a bottom slap! It would have been as useless for me to try and stop Fusae San's laughter, as it was delightful to watch. Maybe there was some hidden understanding or connection between Fusae San and her colleague, of which I was not aware; but, in any case, such innocent humour was refreshing to witness. Almost an inversion to the humour of a loss of dignity is the humour of "self deprecation". In some cases this is applauded but it was not successful in Mark's talk. The audience did not appreciate imagining the speaker in an embarrassing position. The audience did not see the funny side to it; and, indeed, probably felt sorry for him. Bewilderment and personal perplexity are also a kind of self deprecation, and may often be the reason for humour. In Japan this is present in their Manga, or comic cartoons, where characters may often be seen in a dilemma, wildly scratching their heads, although the solution to their problem is in front of them for the whole world to see. The puzzled character in a Manga cartoon can't see the solution, but it is clearly obvious to everyone else, and it is that which makes the situation amusing.

Laughing at the obvious

Among my personal situations, I remember finding it not at all amusing to know that the answer to "What happens if a stork does not stand up?", is simply—"It falls down!". There was riotous merriment to this among my Japanese companions because I didn't appreciate the joke. At another time, someone chuckled himself into fits of laughter because I couldn't adequately explain why parallel railway lines came together in the distance. And yet, when I told the same person, several days later, that a certain British officer who had been recorded as commissioned in 1041 instead of 1941 had applied for the payment of his back pay, it hadn't even raised a smile. Was there too much respect here for the institution, rather than the individual? There is no doubt that humour is a difficult subject to understand. Accounts of my adventures at tea ceremonies, parties, and elsewhere were often subject to much humorous analysis at the Miyazaki's. Not content with my narratives and hearing about it, Emiko would insist on my demonstrating, with actions and tools, just how it happened. When she could see it happening, she had a good hearty laugh. I had to demonstrate how puzzled I was, and then how I had failed to pick up pieces of jelly with my chopsticks; or how I had failed to keep on my straw sandals or waraji, the thongs of which continually slipped from my two big toes around which they should have been firmly secured. It used to cause a lot of fun as I also tried to learn how to do it properly.

Humour from word play and a difference with Emiko

A language like Japanese in which one sound may have several different meanings is also capable of much humorous word play. Japanese lends itself very readily to puns, word witticisms, and often contradictory situations, even more than in English. On several occasions, at weekends or on holidays, two or three of us would go off into the lovely hills of Yamaguchi prefecture, and stay a night at a Japanese hotel or ryokan. At one rather pleasant hotel we were welcomed and greeted by a pretty young kimono clad assistant with the question "koi ni aimashou ka?". That seemed harmless enough. Even I knew that it meant "Would you like to see the gold fish?" and I knew also that many hotels were proud of their aquatic possessions. This particular hotel was possibly a little more jealous of its property than others. Quite innocently, politely, and even encouragingly, I said "Yes, let us do that. Where are they?"; and we were led to a pretty little sunken pool situated a little way inside the hotel, in which truly there were indeed lots of little fish swimming around enjoying themselves. Suddenly there was quite a lot of laughter and I understood. "The penny dropped as we say", and I realised that "Koi ni aimashou ka?" could also be translated as "Would you like to make love?". It was harmless enough, I thought. We all took it as a joke, enjoyed watching the fish, and I thought no more of it. Unfortunately, when I discussed the occasion later with Emiko, she said that hotels which indulged in such humour were probably not of a very high standing, and should be avoided. She thought the question by the hotel was a bad joke, and that it could have led to something entirely different. On reflection, I suppose there may well have been an ulterior motive in the question. I don't know but, In any case, we did receive very good service at the hotel. It was a Sunday, and a lovely warm and sunny afternoon, high up in the hills of Yamaguchi, and it is that which I preferred to remember. Furthermore, the Iwakuni Police chief, Chiefy, about whom I wrote earlier, later recovered for me, from this self same hotel, the silver plated cigarette case which I had bought in India, and which, in that week end, I happened to leave behind when we left. I would be very reluctant to defame the hotel if I could help it. Throughout the whole of my stay in Japan, I was determined, if I could, to avoid misunderstandings. With Emiko, I always had an overriding sense of goodwill and friendship and there was certainly never any chance of a rift between us over the episode. We "laughed it off" very successfully. But, it shows that one needs to be careful. As regards deliberately trying to be funny, or trying deliberately to introduce humour, by making weak jokes, it is probably best not to try. I feel that humour is a subject probably best left to professionals. From my experience, it is probably best of all when it happens spontaneously.

Chapter 23

The Cultural Society and The Status of Women

A perennial topic

From the first Society meeting I ever attended, it was clear that the "Status of women" in Japan would become the society's most controversial topic. At a subsequent meeting, the Society agreed the principle of equal rights for men and women, and voted to work hard for it. Their reason for this was probably a desire to be seen to agree with the views of the Allied Occupation rather than any innate belief in equal rights. Except for one dissentient voice, which penetrated menacingly through the "Ays" of all the others, the whole meeting joined in the popular chorus. Some members, in their eagerness to gain favour, even proffered two hands in voting rather than one. Some had half risen from their hard worn seats and leaned forward over the laps of their compatriots. It might have been a celebration, a general amnesty, or the reading of Caesar's will; enthusiasm was so high. However, it was a very vague commitment by the society, which two members, who had just arrived, immediately and very vividly, revealed. At that very moment, as if to disprove the members' professed beliefs for which they had just voted, we all witnessed a perfect example of their true belief. Nothing could have been more convincing of what was really believed than the scene which, suddenly and unexpectedly, confronted us.

A living example of inequality

A middle aged couple, who were obviously well practised in their long standing custom of inequality, suddenly arrived in full view of the meeting. The man, walking typically a few steps ahead of his wife, entered the hall, kicked his shoes from under his feet, glanced meaningfully between his wife and his shoes, and boldly walked away towards his friends. His wife gracefully lowered herself to her knees, made a beautifully slave like gesture, as only Japanese women know how, and from the folds of her kimono took out a dirty piece of paper which she had obviously used many times before. She carefully wrapped up her husband's shoes in the paper, and then moved quietly to the back of the hall. It would have been sheer hypocrisy or childish stupidity for anyone in the audience to believe that the behaviour we had just witnessed was consistent, in any way, with the equal rights we had only a moment ago been talking about. And yet no one, including even the society's committee members sitting at the top table, seemed to have noticed anything out of place with what we had discussed. None of the women there thought that there was anything wrong or deplorable in the behaviour of our two latest arrivals. For me, it was bitterly disappointing. I was forlorn. No less disappointing at the end of the meeting was the attitude of the younger male members of the audience who like children suddenly jumped up from their benches, shouted a quick Sayonara (good bye), and left the meeting. The ladies were left behind to remove the benches and chairs, and generally to tidy up the hall for school next day. Far from feeling hurt at their treatment, these ladies resisted any overtures to help. They believed it was their duty, and indeed their right, to do any required domestic work of this kind. It looked to me as if it would be only by degrees that we would ever bring about the changes in behaviour which we dearly wanted to see.

A Challenge to Western views

The subject was raised again at the next meeting of the society when we four foreign members of the Society expressed our surprise and dismay at what had happened. We pointed that it was by means unmanly to help in moving heavy furniture. In Western eyes, it was chivalrous and gallant to help anyone, man or woman, who was weaker than us. It seemed at first that we had made a few converts. A few male members did stay behind after our meeting and helped us with moving some of the benches and tables. Unfortunately, our delight was short lived. The cost of making a few converts to our cause was too high. The number of male members in the Society continued to drop. The reluctance to move furniture was similar to the resistance we sometimes met at home in the UK, when we asked young boys and youths to serve tea, or to take up sewing. They felt they were being de-graded and asked to do unmanly things. In the present case, some youngsters were obviously so upset at the way things were going that, rather than try to change their minds and behaviour, they preferred to stop coming to meetings. The voice of a young woman who, in reply to my arguments, remarked almost in total disbelief, "But, surely, you don't expect our men to move furniture, do you?" still echoes in my ears. "They have more important things to do". It was therefore with some trepidation that I later accepted a request to give a talk on the subject. It was agreed that I should call my talk "The Average British Housewife". It was also agreed that I should give the talk in a couple of week's time; and that, rather than having two talks in one evening, the whole meeting would be devoted to just the one subject.

Preparations for a talk

I worked hard during the next two weeks listening to as many ideas and suggestions from my colleagues and Japanese friends as I could. I could hardly claim that my talk was copyright because I had consulted so many people on it. Unfortunately, I was unable to discuss the talk with Emiko and the Miyazaki's until after I had given it. The Miyazaki's had been very helpful on previous occasions but, for various domestic reasons, I was unable to see them during these particular two weeks. They may well have saved me from one or two statements which I made about Japanese domestic economics but, as will be seen, I got through these difficulties fairly amicably. I ended up with four foolscap sheets of closely typed text which Omori San in the typing pool had kindly typed out for me, and which later Shizue then, as always, had very kindly translated for me, writing out the result in beautiful kanji and finally binding it into book form, which I have kept to this very day. So I was very well served indeed. I felt that some people may have thought that, as a very young bachelor with no experience of housewifery, I was wrongly chosen to give the talk. But my audience was very kind as they listened long, silently, and patiently to what I had to say. Shizue again helped me enormously by intervening at appropriate points in my talk to make a translation. At the end of my talk, everyone applauded in an encouraging fashion, and I was besieged with questions.

Chapter 24

Talk on the Average British Housewife

Main points

By way of an introduction to my talk I began by saying how happy I was whenever, in some given situation, I found that men and women were observing equal rights. This I hoped would set the tone for my talk. In such a situation (and marriage should always be one of them), everything then seemed "right with the world". Marriage after all, I said, is where the life of a housewife begins. I went on to say that In Britain, there was no "o-mia" or "arranged marriage", as there was in Japan; when, in 1946, it was still very much the prevailing custom. Consequently, unlike Japan, we had no formal "Nakodo San" or "Go between", whose function it was to bring bride and bridegroom together, sometimes for the very first time. In the UK, parents did of course still have an important influence on events. Indeed, in 1946, in theory at least, it was still the UK custom for the suitor of a young bride to ask the bride's father for permission to marry his daughter. The bride's parents, too, were usually even now responsible for footing the bill for the wedding arrangements, possibly a hangover custom from the days when the bride had to bring a dowry with her. Even in the West, it had taken us some considerable time to make what we believed were desirable changes. Like us, Japan could not expect changes to take place overnight. Making changes would take time and patience. But once the guiding principle of equal rights between men and women was established, the rest would surely follow.

Freedom of choice

At that time, i.e. in 1946, in the UK, two young people having courted, and learned each other's ways and temperament, were usually completely free to declare whom they wanted to marry. It was a fifty-fifty contract. No longer did a woman have to say that she would obey her husband. She normally said, instead, that she will love, honour, and cherish him. Love for each other was the principal factor. Next in importance, in Britain for a housewife, was the home. The home in Britain, as in all countries, was revered and cherished. This feeling was well reflected in the song, "There is no place like home!". Japan's equivalent sentiment had been, and still was, its love for "<u>furusato</u>", the place of one's birth and upbringing. From the moment a young wife in the UK walked down the aisle in the church, to the music of "Here comes the bride", she was dreaming of her home and what she would make of it. At this stage, she was a Queen. She was not now a "slave to the kitchen sink", as she was in the olden days. From her husband's pocket or <u>purse</u> she now had access to lots of today's labour saving devices, electric cookers, washing machines, and so on. Often, the housewife had the main say on <u>domestic issues,</u> and <u>how money should be spent</u>. She was often a Chancellor of the Exchequer, Prime Minister, and Parliament all in one, and sometimes was not a very liberal Government. On <u>children</u> too, the housewife had a very big say in children's upbringing. She was responsible for her child's routine manners, and behaviour. Papa would be called only when baby was naughty and a firm hand was needed. As regards <u>employment</u>, the situation was changing as a result of the war. Before the War, the average housewife did not go to work outside the home. She used to supervise and manage life in the home. During the war, many housewives were called on by the Government to work in factories, offices, and shops, and also to work on farms, where previously they had hardly ever been seen. This pattern had continued to some extent; but, at least in 1946, most women still preferred to be at home as in the pre-war days. I went on to discuss briefly women in independent roles such as politics as well as UK laws relating to inheritance and divorce.

It was noticeable that, in divorce cases in the UK, it was usually women who were given custody of the children.

Differing customs continue

Towards the end of my talk, I ran fairly quickly through other, perhaps less important, customs which were found in our two countries. In Britain, it seemed to me that men looked up to women much more than they did in Japan. It was reflected in the custom of offering one's seat in a crowded bus or train to a woman; or, when entering a room or a building, bowing, and persuading her to enter before a man. There was here perhaps a feeling of chivalry, gallantry, and even *a* protective instinct in doing this. Women were after all generally weaker than men. It was an attitude which I thought would have appealed to Japanese men because of the wonderful tales of the samurai in old Japan, with their magnificent code of honour and loyalty and determination to do good turns. In Japan too, some of the world's first and best authors and novelists were women writers, like Murasaki Shikibu in the 11th century. One might have thought that this would have led to more gallantry by Japanese men,—especially if, for a moment, we compare her,—say with Jane Austen in the UK who only came to fame many years later. Another noticeable difference was that when a man and wife in Japan were out together, the man usually walked ahead of his wife. In Britain, man and wife walked side by side; sometimes arm in arm; sometimes hand in hand. At birth, daughters were welcomed into families just as much as boys. Both were loved equally from the cradle. This was still not true in all countries of course. In Japan I had been terribly disappointed only a few days earlier to read that some girls in Japan had not been allowed to climb a sacred mountain, because it was claimed they would pollute it. Possibly, this was a rare case of inadvertent discrimination; but, in the UK, we would never discriminate between boys and girls in such a way, using such strong language. On discrimination in the UK, there was generally still discrimination in clubs and in some social activities in Britain in 1946, but this was becoming rarer each year. It often took time to change long established customs; and, in some cases e.g. for political voting rights, they had literally to be "fought for". Lastly, I felt that it was worth adding, that British women, even when they were housewives, were often still very active in Sport. They were doing well in Tennis and Golf, and, even in flying aeroplanes.

Questions in abundance

I sensed that there were far fewer men in the audience for my talk than was usually the case and, of those who were there, they seemed more interested in the statutory aspects of marriage and in the rights of men and women in cases of death and divorce, than in simply talking about equal rights. Question time was beginning to test the limited knowledge of both myself and my colleagues, and we seemed to be becoming much too solemn and mournful. Mercifully, the women in the audience were delightfully less legally minded than the men; and the half hour which followed was one of the most entertaining and enjoyable I had ever spent in the company of foreigners. Wit and laughter followed in full measure and "in their five minutes of freedom" I realised that Japanese women could be as tough in argument as their sisters in the West. With some sparkling raillery and spirited attacks, their usual modesty, and their occasionally beautiful withdrawals in their art of defence they almost completely disarmed us. Not all my points were discounted by any means. Despite my being a man, and unmarried at that, my views were not disputed. They were listened to politely. It was only at my criticism of the utter dependency of Japanese women on their men folk, which they fearlessly attacked. The women in the audience were divided roughly into two halves, those who denied that they were treated as inferior and those who didn't deny it, but defended it. It was not so much in open debate but often, privately and quietly afterwards, that I was approached by both sides, "But you don't really understand Sumisu San,—Okusan ga, saifu no himo wo nigirimasu!" (We actually control the Purse strings!)". They almost whispered in my ear. "We also have our "Heso kuri" (literally, our belly button savings), for use in emergencies, over which our husbands have no control whatsoever. Our husbands really know nothing about it." All the women present seemed very proud to have this little bit of sovereignty in the home. Except for this limited amount of sovereignty, which I believed they probably valued rather too highly, it still seemed to me indisputable that at least some Japanese housewives were, unfortunately, and undoubtedly, very much at the whim and mercy of their husband.

Alone with my thoughts

As I rode back that night on my bicycle over the bumpy lanes of Iwakuni towards the camp, I felt that I had in some small way contributed to some new Japanese thought which was now, in any case, beginning to emerge. Although there had been much laughter and good natured banter during the evening, I realised that I had raised some revolutionary ideas into Japanese thinking. I was glad that my arguments had been contested, and not sheepishly accepted, because that meant that they would be remembered and thought about again, and Japanese people would continue to think about them long after I had gone. It was only by degrees and goodwill, that Western ideas regarding women would be accepted and followed. Our ideas could not, and should not, be forced on anybody. The emancipation of women was probably the primary purpose of our attendance at the Society and our lectures; but what indeed is culture if women indeed are not free? It was because we felt so deeply about this, and because the Society was giving us all such an excellent opportunity to meet and understand the Japanese people, that I worked for and continued my membership of the society, right until the day I left for home.

CHAPTER 25

AN UNEXPECTED VISIT TO TOKYO

Out of the Blue

It was in late June, or in early July, 1946, and our Air Officer Admin (AOA) had just called me in to say that AVM Bouchier wanted me to take something personally to the headquarters of the American Military Government (AMG) in Tokyo. In view of the difficulty of other forms of transport across the country at the time, the AVM was very happy for me make use of his own private Dakota, solely for the purpose. I could hardly believe my ears, but I was elated at the opportunity to visit Japan's historic capital. To be able to visit Tokyo so soon after the end of the war was beyond my wildest dreams. But strangely (as it now seems) I didn't ask for more information about the visit. It was just another job. I had been asked to deliver something, and temporarily at least, I was a courier. Nor, did it seem strange to me that I should be asked to take whatever it was directly into General MacArthur' headquarters. I didn't ask for any information about what it was I would be taking. What was it? Who was it for? Why me, when there were now many officers in our HQ of my rank? At that age, I suppose, I did just what I was told. I do not even remember having the grace, either before or after the visit, to thank the AVM for letting me use his own private jet, although I am sure that I must, most certainly,

Chapter 25: An Unexpected Visit To Tokyo

have done so. As I explained in the Preface to my book, I have no documentation written about the visit, either at the time of it, or soon afterwards. In my frequent and almost daily notes, which I received from Emiko, there are references to my visit asking how much I had enjoyed it. Lt. Aizawa, to whom I referred in Chapter 1, (kindness in India) who had been a Japanese Prisoner of War whom I had befriended in India just after the war, also claimed many times later that he had seen me being driven in a jeep in Tokyo about that time. I have no way of knowing whether he really did see me, but anything that might have happened during that magical visit was, I now feel, perfectly possible. I do remember that, on the night before I left for Tokyo, news of my trip had caused quite a stir in the Officers' Mess. I was envied and quizzed as to what the visit was all about, but I was unable to give anyone a very satisfactory answer. It was suggested rather facetiously that, as a quid pro quo, I should ask the AMG for the return of some of the utensils and crockery which they had taken with them when they left,—because we were still short of western type utensils for eating. I said that, if there was an opportunity for me to raise the matter diplomatically, I would try to do this. Many years on, I now regret that I did comply with this request. This is because, although the request was in one sense very successful, I do not believe that it was a very wise thing for me to do. In fact, it was rather silly. My reason for believing this will become clearer later.

My job as one time Courier

When I saw the shape and size of whatever it was I was to take to Tokyo, I could not help but wonder what it was. It was too big to be described as a packet or a parcel, or even a small box. It was more like a little crate. It was awkward to carry but I had still been asked to keep it beside me for the whole time I was on the aircraft. I came to the conclusion that possibly it was some sort of secure communications equipment which perhaps several months earlier the American Forces had left behind by mistake, that is, when they had handed the station over to us in BCOF. Presumably, the equipment had only now been discovered. At any rate, this explanation must have satisfied my initial curiosity since afterwards I hardly thought any more about it. After reflecting on the situation and some of the circumstances prevailing at the time, however; and now, particularly when writing about my visit,

- 155 -

I have been wondering whether there might not have been perhaps a little more significance to my visit to Tokyo than I had realised. At the end of the chapter, under the heading of "Reflections on the visit", I will discuss these musings in a little more detail.

The AVM's Private Jet

I was certainly very privileged to be the only passenger aboard our AVM's private jet aircraft, into which I clambered with my goods one morning after breakfast. There were only three of us in the plane, the AVM's two personal aircrew and me. My "cargo" was beside me throughout the flight and I remember leaning over it a little later, rather awkwardly, to get a superb view of Mt Fuji, as we majestically flew past it at a slightly higher height than the mountain itself. It was a marvellous sight, of which the Japanese people are rightly very proud, and it is one which I have long remembered. We were met at the Airport in Tokyo by a representative from the UK Liaison Office, since the British Embassy had not yet re-opened after the War. As far as I can remember, it was by now mid afternoon and I was taken out later for a modest evening meal in a local restaurant. Again there was no mention made of what the contents were in the package which I was bringing with me, other than to say we would be delivering it the next morning, personally as directed, into General MacArthur's HQ in the AMG's offices on the sixth floor of the famous "Dai Ichi" building in Tokyo. Many years later, this building has become a very impressive national museum, holding a large number of historical and priceless records of Wartime and Post War Japan. I wonder if my visit is recorded there.

General MacArthur's HQ

The next morning I was taken by Jeep with my "cargo" to AMG HQ; and, for my benefit, we took a marvellous roundabout route to see a little bit of Tokyo, where presumably Lt. Aizawa may have seen me. Driving in a jeep, so soon in the Occupation, through the streets of Tokyo was all too wonderful for words. In the course of handing over my mysterious goods to two or three United States officers in the AMG HQ, I believe I saw General MacArthur (SCAP—Supreme Commander Allied Powers) as he walked through the room in which we were sitting; but, if I did, I was not invited to speak with him. The officers, who were with me, and who were of quite high rank, said they were very interested to know about the early work of BCAIR and its achievements, and this led to some vague discussion about circumstances there, and the effect on us of the anti-fraternisation policy. I said that I thought that fraternisation had helped us to achieve our aims, especially in winning the support of the local population, at a time when we were imposing on them some extremely harsh conditions. I was told that the main reason for introducing an anti fraternisation policy had been to combat black market activity, which was becoming very rife in the country. When I asked what was General MacArthur's personal attitude towards fraternisation I was told that, other things being equal, the general's preference would be "to let nature take its course",—which seemed pretty close to my own views. Such an opinion also seemed contrary to what we were all being told officially in Iwakuni, so I did not mention it when I got back to BCAIR. I was asked by AMG if they could do anything for us, in return for my bringing them the package which I had delivered. After a certain amount of banter and good humour, this seemed an opportunity for me to ask if it was possible for AMG to return some of our Officers' Mess crockery and utensils which US troops had taken with them when they had left Iwakuni,—particularly as we were still rather short of these. This request was what my fellow officers in BCAIR had asked me to make. I did it as diplomatically as I could, and a week or so later, lo and behold, a supply of this much needed equipment did arrive in our Mess. This seemed like success; my request had been granted. On reflection, however, I wish I had never made it, because I feel that the request may have been regarded, not least by General MacArthur, as flippant; and certainly not something he would have wanted to talk to me about.

A stroll in the Ginza

On the way back to the UK Liaison Mission, I was thrilled when my companion parked the jeep in the famous Ginza area and invited me to get out and walk around. For me, it was a moment of history. Very few BCAIR personnel could have enjoyed such a valuable experience during their stay in Japan as I did at that moment. As one might have expected, there was more activity and life in Tokyo than there was in Iwakuni. There were more temporary shops and stalls alongside the road open for business, and more people spending money; but there were none of today's large and prosperous department stores. Instead, I could see a lot of bomb damage, buildings in a state of disrepair, and evidence of bomb destruction in many places. The Ginza was alive, if only in anticipation of better things to come, but it was nowhere near as lively as the very busy, bustling, and thriving Ginza of today. I also remember being surprised at seeing one or two jinrikisha (rickshaws) taking people about their business. Now, 66 years on this is perhaps hard to believe; but, just after the war, transport was by no means cheap or easy to obtain. It all seems very strange now that I was never questioned, either by our AOA or AVM, about my experiences during these two very eventful days and that they never told me of any results of the visit which may have been reported to them. I simply assumed, following the dictum that "no news is good news", that the visit must have been deemed successful.

Reflections on the visit

In the summer of 1946, after I had been to Tokyo, I was not at all concerned about my visit. As instructed, I had done my job as a courier; and, as asked, I had delivered some goods in person to AMG in Tokyo. I had done the job, and I had enjoyed immensely the travel which went with it. I was not asked for a report on the visit and hence I didn't make one, other than to sign a formal note that I had delivered the goods safely. Now, 66 years on, after looking a little more closely at some of the unusual aspects of the visit, I have a better appreciation of the situation at the time, and also, just possibly, a reason why I was chosen to undertake the visit in the first place. The two most important features of my visit were undoubtedly (i), our AVM's vey kind decision to let me have the sole use of his private plane to take me to Tokyo and back, and (ii), the instruction which I was given to "make sure" that I delivered whatever it was that I was taking, personally and directly, into the AMG's offices. It was an instruction which I and my escort from the UK Mission carried out faithfully to the letter. A third and interesting feature of the situation was that just a little while before my visit, I had written a paper for AVM Bouchier on the progress which BCAIR had been making on the build up of its forces. I had stressed that we had made very good progress in building up BCAIR's strength while, at the same time, we had maintained extremely good

Chapter 25: An Unexpected Visit To Tokyo

relations with the local population. We had also done this, despite the harsh requisitioning work, the labour enforcement policy, and other conditions, which we were sometimes imposing on the people at the time. I had also commented in the paper, on how fraternisation had helped us in our work, as well as on the issue of equal rights for men and women (as per the two preceding chapters). It was interesting that General MacArthur, the Supreme Allied Commander in Japan at the time, was known to be a strong advocate of women's rights. It had been largely due to General MacArthur that women's suffrage was now guaranteed in Japan's National Constitution. It is possible (or, at least, I like to think it is) that AVM Bouchier may have agreed with what I had written and, assuming that he was possibly having regular discussions with AMG, he may have said that AMG, and possibly even General MacArthur himself, would like to know what I had written, perhaps in view of my being selected for a post with the Occupation Forces, rather like that of Hank whom I mentioned in Chapters 2 and 5. As I would be passing through their offices, when I delivered whatever it was I was bringing, AMG might just care to see me. When the "plan", if it ever was a plan, had fallen flat, however, and I had not even spoken with General MacArthur, our AVM may well have felt that I had let him down. This may have prompted him to write later in his otherwise very complimentary letter about me, to which I referred at the end of the first paragraph of Chapter 5, that I was "not always impressive in an interview". This was a little strange because I am sure that at no time was I ever formally interviewed by him. Much of the above is of course pure speculation. There is no firm evidence for it. It probably didn't happen at all as I have written it; but it is, I believe, just plausible. We will never know. What I do know is that whatever happened regarding my Tokyo visit, AVM Bouchier, by writing his very favourable letter about me, without ever being asked to do so, had never let me down—right up to the very end of my stay in Japan. On the other hand; I am afraid it could be that, during my visit to Tokyo, I may well have been the very one to have let him down.

Chapter 26

With the Miyazaki's at the Pictures

The danger of taking risks

Peter was much more like Jock in his attitude towards official directives, as well as to public reaction, than I was; and hence he was much less cautious than me. He was due to leave Japan a lot sooner than I was, and that may possibly have made a difference. I was worried about being too rash, not so much because I was in fear of physical consequences to me but because any recklessness on my part would almost certainly end my contacts and friendship with Japanese families. However, I didn't have strong enough will to avoid the risks for very long; and, hence during one lazy summer afternoon, Peter, Emiko, her mother, and I, could be seen walking along the new river bank, which had recently been developed, towards the Iwakuni cinema, a half of which the Miyazaki's owned. I recall even now the scene of the four of us, ambling alongside the river in full view of the main bridge and of the High street through which a lot of traffic was passing. Emiko was dressed as if in deference to us, in a very bright and most becoming white European dress, with a blue collar and cuffs, and a red belt round her waist. She had a highly coloured sunshade across her shoulders which left a wealth of beautifully uncovered hair that could be seen under a halo of sunlight. The sun was blazing

Chapter 26: With the Miyazaki's at the Pictures

down relentlessly from a blue sky; and yet Emiko, as always, was so cool and fresh beneath her sunshade, and so full of the goodness of life. Just to look at her was sheer joy. Mrs Miyazaki, at the other side of me, was dressed in a much more sombre and solemn coloured kimono, providing a happy balance to Emiko's youthful display. All this was wonderful, until I had a sudden sense of unease. Suddenly, I realised that we were in the full public gaze and that this could spoil everything. My fears were undoubtedly noticed by my companions. I was fidgety and looking around to see who was watching us. Instead of being proud of two delightful ladies, mother and daughter, who had so kindly invited us to an afternoon of novel entertainment; it seemed as if I was ashamed of their company. Nothing could be further from the truth, but I was terribly troubled because what I was doing was doubly wrong. I was risking the happiness of both Mrs Miyazaki and Emiko, which I longed for most sincerely; while, at the same time, I was contravening the new anti-fraternisation polices of our Armed Forces, which I always wished to serve as loyally and faithfully as I could. In the midst of this ecstasy of a lovely summer's afternoon in Japan, it was mental anguish. It was torture, and it was cruel. How could it be that, in Japan, where it was possible to find such joy, there could also be such pain? As Robert Browning had once written, it was "a paradox comforting while it mocked".

Worries are temporarily overcome

Despite my inner feelings, I was determined to make the afternoon a success. Temporarily at least, I put aside my worries and began to enjoy the day. We followed the river for a while, and then turned under a railway bridge into a fairly crowded area of shops and dwellings until we reached a building which was standing out larger than the rest. In front of it, there was a small square in which people were gathering and chatting, while also looking at various posters, advertisements, and forthcoming attractions. The building was of course the cinema. Without being told, or if not knowing Japanese, one might never have guessed what it was. It might have been anything from a factory to a hospital. The Japanese people had no airs about it being a cinema. Most people there were bemused by the appearance of two British officers in the company of two Japanese ladies, but there was certainly no hostility towards us. Indeed, after a little while, it was all extremely

Memoires of Japan 1946

friendly. The management were even more hospitable, due possibly to the presence of the wife of one of the owners. We were ushered in by the commissionaire and two uniformed usherettes, past the cash desk into a lobby where, after much smiling, bowing, and gesticulating, we were required to remove our foot ware. With that done, we were directed up some polished wooden stairs, on to the balcony. As I glanced back, while climbing the stairs silently in our stockinged feet, I caught an enquiring look in the manager's eyes, "To what" he must have been thinking "does my humble cinema owe such an honoured visit?" At least I always felt he was the manager by his attitude, but he was very casually dressed, wearing army khaki drill trousers and an open necked, short-sleeved, civilian shirt. We took our seats in the centre at the front of the balcony. There were also people in the wings, as well as, below and in front, of us, much like a cinema at home in England. There were no chairs. We threw our arms round our knees and sat as comfortably as we could on the soft straw matted floor, or tatami. Peter for once looked awkward, but I felt quite content as I surveyed the scene before me. Emiko, in her good natured way, was exuberant and intent on telling me everything. I don't think I had ever heard her so eager to speak before. Mrs Miyazaki was saying little. The building was of unpainted wood, and due probably to the general economic situation after the war, was in need of repair. In design, it was very much like an English cinema. It even went so far as to have a clock at one side of the screen, and an advertisement for next week's attraction, on the other.

The film begins

Before the film began, the hubbub inside the cinema was deafening. It reached a crescendo just as the lights were gradually lowered indicating that the film was about to begin. The title of the film was "Aizen katsura" which might be translated as "The lovers' tree", the Katsura being the lovely so called Japanese Judas tree, on which pretty purple flowers blossom before the leaves appear. It was a sentimental film, portraying the lives of two young Japanese lovers, a doctor and a nurse, who were intent on marriage to each other. Unfortunately, the very pretty young nurse was considered by the doctor's parents to be below their class in society, and so the nurse was forbidden by them to marry their son. The audience was in tears. Both men and women were continually wiping their eyes, gulping down their sobs to stem the flow, and very nearly half choking themselves in the attempt. I had never heard such stifled outbursts of pathos before, but it rumbled on and on like a dirge. However, I was amused by it; and, at one point, I was almost rebuked by Emiko for not paying heed to her explanations. I was aware none the less of the very deep feelings being generated by the film. I was convinced then, as I always had been, of how strong the emotions of the Japanese people can be, whether shown passively in tears or in more physical ways. Once moved by this spirit or feeling, they often think back to their own history of a long line of heroes and legends. They think of their daimyo and samurai, of which they are justifiably very proud. I was disappointed that I didn't always understand all the dialogue of the film, although in my own defence I felt that the sound system there was not all that it might have been, due to presumably to economic conditions. Furthermore, with all due respect to the actors, I was often more interested in the activity of live audience than I was in the imitation of life on the screen. Even when I followed the dialogue, I often liked to have an explanation from Emiko to confirm my translation. Peter was at first intrigued by it all, but he grew restless; and, before the end, I also felt uncomfortable. We were after all sitting in unusually cramped positions. As the lights went up we were told that what we had just seen was the first part of the film and that the second part would be shown next week. This serial form of showing films was popular in Japan with fans and critics alike, enabling them to discriminate between the two performances. Peter and I were glad to be relieved of our crouching positions. Our backs were aching. Mine felt as if it was permanently arched for life, and Peter's, he said, was just as if it had been severed in two. We made as if we were ready to leave but this we realised later was a mistake. Our eagerness to leave had seemingly offended our hosts. Both Emiko and her mother, unusually for them, had pained expressions, and explanations from Emiko about the film, which previously had been so plentiful, suddenly ceased.

Local customs must be observed

Most of the audience had remained in their seats. Some were still dolefully wiping tears from their eyes, some with handkerchiefs, some with the sleeves of their kimonos, and among the men, some with their

European neckties. The audience had cried continuously for over two hours, and it seemed that after a few minutes they wanted to start again. To judge by the complacent look of the manager; as he surveyed his future unprofitable patrons, it was not only their right for them to sit through the film again, it was also a national custom. Apparently, some people would stay for three or four showings of the film and then go home afterwards at the same time as the management. Our very brisk, all too prompt, standing up—and maybe the odd yawn was quite out of touch with what was expected from us. The same could be said of our conspicuous limb stretching exercises as we recovered ourselves. Of course, neither Peter nor I had the remotest wish to slight our hosts or to appear casual about the film in any way. Indeed, very much to the contrary, we both wanted to appear extremely grateful to our hosts for providing us with such good entertainment which, except for a few superficial aches and pains, we had thoroughly enjoyed. Probably we could have expressed our gratitude better, by remaining in our seats eager to see the film again; but, in our western minds, such a thought just didn't occur to us. Although there was mutual long standing good will between the Miyazaki's and us, this had been a very brief period of misunderstanding. It made me realise more than ever that it is only after the bitter experience of error that we learn all the niceties and finesse which are necessary for the real understanding of a people. A perfect knowledge of the language helps, but it is only half way. Any rupture between us in this particular case was soon repaired. We regained our shoes, returned the bows and smiles of the manager, and then good humouredly took our leave. I tried to scratch away the veneer which we westerners always place on any country; but, I found that I still believed in romantic Japan, with all its mythical characters, its children's heroes, and its brave samurai, with their code of love and honour, and with hearts just as emotionally charged and human, as any of our own.

Homeward bound

Conversation about the film continued all the way home. It caused more fun and laughter among us as Peter and I tried to describe how the West, and particularly the Americans, might have portrayed the story. In the film we had just seen, there was no embracing, no sighs or pangs of love, no kisses, and no leg or body scenes, of which in our films there probably would have been a great deal. As Peter said there wasn't even a handshake. Yet, had it been desired, there was also plenty of opportunity in the film for many serious expressions of passion and amour. We were left in no doubt that the Japanese people did not relish the change to Western ideas and, very conservatively, would resist them. However, there was little doubt that in the end, not only the film industry, but in real life too, many shocking "western practices" were going to replace those we had just seen. Even the subject of the film, which in fact was really about "free love" in a country which still recognised "o miai" (the arranged Marriage) and the "Nakadou San" (the Go between), was quite an innovation. We all agreed that more similarities would follow. American films, perhaps with appropriate cuts, were already being seen in large cities throughout the world. English sound tracks replaced by Japanese dialogue, would inevitably find their way soon into Japan. It was only a matter of time. No Sunday Observation Society, or Board of Censors, would be able to stop it. I didn't pretend to imagine that all was fine in Japan until the arrival of Commodore Perry in 1853, but I couldn't help feeling that many of Japan's wrong turns did date from that period and very probably could be imputed to the West. In the interests of trade, Japan often imported our faults as well as our good points. Much now depended on the example which we in the Occupation Force, in our behaviour, were setting for Japan to follow. But, suddenly, I noticed that my three companions were not even listening to my woolly thoughts and platitudes. They were talking and laughing quite happily, leaving me almost isolated; as we approached the Miyazaki's home.

End of a fascinating visit

I would have loved nothing better than to accept the Miyazaki's invitation to tea. We were implored to enter their home but I looked at my watch and it was already after four o'clock. I was also a truant, and on my advice we declined the splendid offer. Of course, I regretted it for the rest of the evening, and so I believe did Peter because he never took my advice again. He would go to Emiko's even when I deemed it unwise. We had returned to the office to find that we had not been missed. No one had called us. We sat down to tea and listened to various bits of dull information and felt thoroughly miserable. It was an anti climax to an excellent afternoon. I went to my room, sat on

Memoires of Japan 1946

my bed, and sighed. If only I could do in Japan all that I wanted to do. So much was denied to my inquisitive spirit. But it was no use. The Japanese people had the very apt expression, "shikata ga nai"—there is nothing you can do about it, and there really wasn't. I looked at the photograph which my room girl, Fusae San, had long ago put in a frame at my bedside. It was a splendid photograph of the heroine we had just seen in the film! It was typical of the way in which fate likes to play a part in our lives.

Chapter 27

Final Days and Fond Farewells

A time to leave

When the news of my departure date from Japan was announced at the end of the Japanese summer, I was very tempted to consider applying for an extension to stay on a little longer in Japan, because I had been so very happy throughout the whole of the seven months I had been there. The prospects were not particularly good, however. The war was now over; and, in order to reduce its costs, the UK Government was anxious to repatriate and demobilise its forces as fast as it could. On a personal level too, the prospects were not bright. I no longer had the gloriously free rein which, in my early days I had had in Japan, and which, very happily, had also continued for sometime afterwards. Nowadays, my activities were very much more restricted than they used to be. There were huge numbers of senior officers here above me. One step up, to Squadron Leader or Major, was no problem; it seemed we were all much of the same kin. At Wing Commander/ Lt Colonel level we could have the occasional spot of fun; but, as for Group Captains or Colonels, we usually kept them at a distance; except, that is, if they were not principally Service people, but rather specialists like the PMO, BCAIR's Principal medical Officer, whom I liked very much, and with whom I got on extremely well. Above this level, Air Commodore/

Brigadier and above, these ranks were above the stratosphere, and in another world. Yet, in my early days in Japan, I had lived in this world. In addition, and most importantly, I knew I was not going to be at all happy with the new anti-fraternisation laws which would distance me, and perhaps sometimes cut me off completely, from my Japanese activities and friends. Finally, I had been away from my family and friends at home, for nearly three years. At least, back in the UK, to where I would be returning, I had something to look forward to. In the end, I decided not to apply for any extension to my time in Japan, excellent though that time had been. On balance, I thought it was time to leave. And so, instead, I resolved to make the best possible use of my last few days in Japan to meet with, and to say my very sincere and fond goodbyes to, as many of my Japanese friends and acquaintances as I possibly could. I knew that I would probably never have the chance to see many of them, ever again. It was a sad decision.

Formal farewells were not possible

With the Anti fraternisation laws taking hold, and becoming ever more stringently applied, it had become quite impossible for me, or anyone, to arrange and organise any kind of meaningful farewell, to mark the end of my wonderful time in Japan. Had it been humanly feasible, it would have been sheer joy to bring together my Service colleagues, Japanese friends, and families, and all the fine people I had worked with, in helping to get Japan back on its feet after the war. For many of us, and particularly me, it would have been an occasion to savour for a lifetime. My position, in this respect, was very similar to that of my erstwhile, great friend and colleague, Squadron Leader Jock Ogilvie, RAAF, whom I could never forget. Three or four months earlier, Jock had left us to go to Bofu but, even at that time, any extensive farewell mixture of Japanese and Armed Forces company would, quite simply, not have been allowed. The possibility of doing it now, socially and openly, would have been even harder for me than it had been for Jock Ogilvie. The matter was out of the question, and so I began a very sad round of goodbyes.

Individual Goodbyes

Intentionally, I attended the very last possible meeting of the Iwakuni Cultural Society so that I could say goodbye to as many

Chapter 27: Final Days and Fond Farewells

members as possible of the people I had met and knew there. High on my list, was Dr Fujimura, the school headmaster; and, of course, Shizue, who had done so much to help me personally. I also had a final word with several members of the Society who had been prominent in asking me questions, and then standing up so bravely to my assertions. I said goodbye to Mark, who attended a different officer's mess from me. He too would be leaving Japan in a few months time. He gave me a lovely thank you letter of appreciation (written in Japanese) for my contributions to the Society, which was still so very dear to him. I called on Chiefy, the local Police chief, and his interpreter, Mickey, and Kawamura San, the AMG liaison officer, as well as the Mayor's office, to all of whom I expressed my sincere gratitude for the unstinted help they had given me. On another day, I visited the Fukugawa ryokan where in the early days I had had such delightful parties with office personnel, the interpreters, and girls from the typing pool. On that same day, I visited the Aburaya ryokan, where we had held many working meetings; and, afterwards, where we had enjoyed some lovely periods of relaxation. I can still hear in my mind the two owner sisters imploring me as I left, "Come back soon, Sumisu; do please come back". I thanked Captain Brown of the Royal Australian Army, and his Transport office which had provided me, on an untold number of occasions, with a jeep and chauffer. Like Jock, who had left Iwakuni before me, I had always found him a tremendous friend and, strangely, although Australian, far more pro-British in his attitude to everything than we were ourselves. Goodbyes, too, to my New Zealand and Indian counterparts who had not shared many of my meetings with Japanese people; but whose company I had often enjoyed, on trips to the countryside, and on visits to places of interest,—again, always courtesy of our Transport chief, Captain Brown. At the time of saying my goodbyes, memories came flowing back ceaselessly, one after the other, and I treasured them as if they were jewels. I also thanked all the personnel in the guard room, at the main entrance to the camp, who had kept me supplied with a bicycle to ride, whenever I had asked them, which occurred more times than I can count. It was indeed after, very conveniently, borrowing such a useful bicycle, as I had done so often before, that I spent my very last evening in Japan with Emiko at the Miyazaki's.

My last evening with Emiko

It was very sad making what was to be my last visit to the Miyazaki's home, and also alas, my very last evening with Emiko, at least for some considerable time ahead. We didn't know the future. Emiko and I were very fond of each other; but, living thousands of miles apart, we knew that we would not be in command of our futures. We made no promises. There were no hidden pacts, of love, or friendship; but we knew that we were destined to keep in touch. There was every possibility that we would meet again. There was no need to be gloomy, so we sat down and enjoyed a really pleasant evening, as we always had. Emiko played a few last notes on both the koto and the samisen and recited a few Japanese poems; and, for a moment, I re-captured my dreams. How can one be so happy and so sad at the same time? There is something so Japanese in this paradox. We remembered the first time we had met,—at the wonderful party which the girls at the camp had given to us all so long ago, just before the departure of the Australian squadron to Bofu. We reminisced for a long time, over all the many memorable things we had done together, since then; firstly, with Jock, and then with Peter, both of whom had left before me. We exchanged mutual everlasting thanks to each other for the enjoyment we had shared, and we said our goodbyes as profusely as any really good friends ever can. That did not include, as I am sure Jock would have insisted it should, anything like a long, lingering, farewell kiss. That was not the Japanese way. I walked back along the same now familiar magical garden path at the entrance to the Miyazaki home, the path that had so long ago had first bewitched me and which had made my heart beat faster every time I had trodden along it; but, this time, sadly I was very moving away from, and not towards, my heaven. I mounted my bicycle, still waving and shouting my goodbyes, and the Miyazaki's were doing the same for me, as I rode off into the darkness. In one sense, I was dead to the world, but I was conscious enough to be wondering just what did the future hold for both of us. Last of all, at the end of a momentous day, I had a farewell drink with several officers in the Officer's Mess. This was my last friendly goodbye that evening. Then, suddenly, strangely, and unaccountably, as I left the Mess, I became almost overcome by emotion. As my very close friend from Scotland, Mark, might have said, I was probably feeling a wee bit lonely. But it was, also,—alas, the end of a wonderful dream.

Chapter 27: Final Days and Fond Farewells

The last sad morning

I checked the labels on my large metal trunk and other luggage to be collected for my homeward voyage. I said my adieus to my roommate in room 69, the Australian newspaper correspondent, Jack Evans, and to our room girl, Fusae San. Except for those special events, it might almost have been any morning as usual. I had breakfast in the Mess. I went straight up to my desk in the office, and I checked that there was no outstanding work for me. It was a very strange situation. I had been given no information on who was taking over my work; and I had certainly never taken any part in any formal handover of my job. When I left my desk, I might just as well have been going off on some afternoon visit. But, this time there was to be no return. Possibly, it had not yet been decided; or, perhaps some complete re-organisation, unknown to me, was already in the making. I spent a few minutes saying goodbye with the AOA, who was still, nominally at least, my next superior officer; although he was by now still fairly new in his job, our original AOA having left a few weeks earlier. I also spent a few minutes with Air Vice Marshal Bouchier, and thanked him very much indeed for his personal note to me, and the copy of the letter he had so kindly written to my prospective employers in the UK, which his staff officer had given me. He wished me well and good luck in my future career. It was a sad parting in many ways, not because I had been directly involved with him recently, but because I had been so very close to him in those very early days, when everything had been so new and magical; and, so far as my work was concerned, there had been hardly another officer between us. I moved on into the typing pool, and thanked them for all the considerable amount of typing which they had done for me without a single moan, over the past six months, both official work and otherwise. It was all a little dreamlike. I don't think I thought I was really leaving at all. I checked that my luggage had been collected from my room; and, I saw that there was still an hour or more to go before I needed to be at the embarkation point where I would join others, none of whom I really knew; and then, we would then truly be on our way to Kure, and, in several weeks time, I would be home. What better could I do, but stroll down Iwakuni's High street, and call on Mrs Fujimoto? She was delighted to see me, and we had a most enjoyable little chat; and, I had my very last cup of tea in Japan, for a very long time. It was the end of the most important chapter of my life,—at least so far.

Part III

Thoughts on a Memorable Experience

(A case of Introspection)

Chapter 28

A Charmed Existence

Throughout my stay

Looking back now at the period from the moment of my arriving in Japan on March 1st 1946, until the morning I left seven months later at the end of September, I feel as if I had been living a charmed existence. Despite all the harsh human conditions around me, and the obviously terrible sufferings of many Japanese people as a result of the war, all of which affected me greatly, I had an inner peace which I couldn't explain. It seemed that I could do no wrong, nor was it likely that I could fall into any kind of danger. I had had such unlimited freedom of movement and action that, strangely, I felt as if, magically, I was protected from all the perils of life; just as much as I seemed to be protected from the results of my own mistakes and follies. I had walked through the streets of Iwakuni, often alone during the day or night, completely unaware that I might have been attacked by some aggrieved citizen who, for some reason or other, was at odds with the Occupation forces. I had visited Hiroshima several times completely unaware of the dangers to the human body of nuclear radiation, which was still being recorded there. I had gone alone into hotels, businesses and other places, as I would have done back in the UK, without any fear of unpleasant encounters. At work, it seemed that I could do whatever I thought was right without asking for higher approval. Sometimes, I had probably put into action many deeds which were well above my rank to initiate. It had been unbelievable joy to have had such complete freedom, of action and space, as I wished. On the face of things, I wasn't accountable to anybody. I had been more than fortunate in having so many friendly colleagues, especially Squadron Leader Jock Ogilvy, RAAF, who had set me off on the right track in the first place, and Flt Lt. Mark McLaughlin with whom I had also served in Burma and India. From my very earliest days in Japan, I had also been extremely grateful to have had the unfailing support of our highest ranking officer in BCAIR, Air Vice Marshal Bouchier, and also of our Air Officer Administration, both of whom had been silent about some of my more questionable activities, even supposing that that they knew about them. Socially, and without much effort from me, I had had the good fortune to meet some wonderful people and to have enjoyed some very sincere friendships. I had been blessed to see and take part in many fascinating Japanese activities, which hitherto I could only have read about. I had had frequent contact and conversations with important and influential members of a local community, all of whom had displayed a remarkable resilience in showing us all how to recover from a disastrous war. This had included the local police chief, the mayor, and chief educationists, local business people, hoteliers; and, at many enjoyable meetings, the committee and members of the Iwakuni Cultural Society. These good people had all been fine human beings striving hard to find better ways of living together, and the best principles of life to be living by. Above all, I had become very close to two wonderful families with whom I could really relax, and use as a base for viewing and meeting the Japanese people around me. I had met ordinary people, including especially those who were around me all day long at the camp, our room girls, our interpreters, office staff, our kitchen staff, and all the many others who had helped to make our lives so pleasant to be living. It was magic then; and, so is the memory of it, still today.

Influence above rank

It was possibly a stroke of good fortune for me that, during the initial stage of building up BCAIR forces, there had been such a huge gap between my rank as a Flight Lieutenant and our next two senior officers in BCAIR, namely our AVM and AOA. It is true that Squadron Leader Ogilvie had been appointed as my initial guide when I arrived, but he was a member of an RAAF unit, and was not strictly a part of BCAIR. Undoubtedly, the resulting situation; although, I was certainly not aware of it at the time, meant that many requests and suggestions which I made, and opinions which I voiced, appeared to come from the top of our Organisation. Similarly, it was because I had such immediate access to this hierarchy, that it was thought by others that I was personally aware of everything taking place within it. It was also no doubt believed that I was able to report to our most senior officers everything that was happening. This view was held presumably not only by members of BCAIR; but, also by all the people n the community, and especially by many local people with whom I had dealings. My friend, Mark McLaughlin, who had had the same rank as I had at that time, often used to say to me, many years afterwards, that I had never really understood the important influence which I had over people, because of this situation. I knew that our AVM always had a keen interest in Org. 3, my official posting, because he had said that he had personally selected me for it; but, I never imagined that this gave me such influence in my dealings with people. On reflection, it may explain a lot of things about the charmed existence I was living.

Never once rebuked or criticised

Despite, the tremendous amount of work which used to come across my desk as Org. 3; the many instructions I issued; the amount of work which I initiated; the many mistakes I must have made in the continuous turmoil and rush of everyday business; not to mention also the risk of news leaking out about my private escapades; I cannot ever remember being rebuked, criticised, or censored, in any way. It was truly a remarkable experience, the like of which I had never met before, and I have never met since. Early in my service in Japan I had attended a dubious party at the Fukugawa ryokan, as I have described in Chapter 9; and I had listened to the pitiful tale of a geisha. This had led me into an encounter with the Military Police. On the following Monday morning, after an uneasy Sunday pondering my fate, I related the circumstances of this remarkable event to our Chief of Security. After that, I never heard one word more about it, and not even a "do be careful in future!" Towards the end of June, I submitted a report to AVM Bouchier, on the progress we had made in the building up of our forces in BCAIR, which was by then very nearly up to strength. I referred to this report in the last paragraph of Chapter 25, which was about reflections on my unexpected visit to Tokyo. Not a word was ever said to me about my report, although I was surprised when it crossed my desk again a few days later, having been amended by our PR people. The substance of my report had not perhaps been changed but it had been expressed in rather more suitable Civil Service jargon, in the use of which I had not yet been trained. This correction was never discussed with me, and my own version was never criticised. With complete silence on these matters; and, especially, on my meetings socially with Japanese people, and in the light of the increasingly anti-fraternisation policy, which latterly came into force, it is perhaps not surprising that I felt I was living a charmed existence. It was all so unnatural. At times, it was uncanny; but it did lead me to some serious thinking about life.

Lessons in life

I had arrived in Japan in 1946 as a boy. I left exactly seven months later a very much wiser and grown up person, vividly aware not only of the wonderful joys and events which can happily occur in our lives but also of the harsh realities of life, and sometimes inhuman conditions, under which some of us are sometimes called upon to live. I do not pretend that, during those seven months time, I learned all the lessons which there are to be learned in one's lifetime; for, while we live at all, we are always learning. But, within the first few days of my being in Japan, I had been shattered (as I travelled through Hiroshima) by the horrors of war, and the helplessness of mankind in its inability to prevent them. The stomach wrenching evidence was there for all to see, and literally feel. My vivid imagination of its cruelty took my distress further still; and, it was frightening, beyond the words I knew to express it. Hiroshima was the scene of a human disaster. At that time it was, and it still is, beyond human ability to describe it. It remained a frightful reminder to me throughout my stay in Japan, and it was never far from my thoughts. In the months ahead, I was to witness its knock on effects, the anguish of those who had been injured or who had lost their loved ones, as well as the pain of others who now had nothing, and were living in poverty. It was a hard lesson to learn. I had seen at close quarters how the Japanese had coped with their plight fought back from the brink. This was with the same stoicism which they show

Chapter 28: A Charmed Existence

towards Nature, which they worship; but which alas, also ironically has its dreadful earthquakes, its typhoons, and its tsunamis. During my stay in Japan I often had little chats with our interpreters and others, youngsters of my own age or even younger; and, as youngsters will, we would talk about life and its meaning, and why are we here at all, and so forth. I was always impressed how sensitively and sincerely these youngsters believed in the glory and wonder of Nature, and how very touchingly they would express their belief. They would pick up a stray twig, leaf, or stone, or sometimes even a scrap of paper, and say, and really mean it, how wonderful that this should be. Isn't this just magnificent? I do wonder how long in life they held on to these beliefs, especially in the light of some of Nature's own disasters, and the misery which has also followed. But, mercifully, like people all over the world, the Japanese people do still find time, amidst the hardships in life to appreciate the joys of living, and I enjoyed sharing these times with them. I hope I have reflected these times, both happy ones, and also sometimes sad ones, in my writings about them. But, in truth, I could not have had a better start to "growing up"; and, for that, I am eternally grateful.

Chapter 29

Hard to Believe

No direct control or supervision

It still amazes me that I, and others too of course with whom I worked, were able to achieve as much as we did—apparently without any tangible control, or supervision, over what we were doing. So far as our work was concerned, what we were achieving in requisitioning property, in the daily ritual of compulsory labour enforcement, and in controlling local peoples' activities, and so forth, was obvious to everyone in Iwakuni. That this work could be carried out, without any sign of public dispute or argument about it, was more than remarkable; it was almost unbelievable. It must have met with our masters' approval; since, never once, were any complaints about it expressed. It didn't really matter. We did not really need or want congratulations. My particularly social activity, however, was quite different. It is hard to understand why there was never any criticism of it; and, why especially later, when there was such increasing attention being paid to the Occupation Forces' anti-fraternisation policy, my superiors, apparently, didn't know of my activities; or, if they did, why they never said anything about them to me. I would have expected at least some warning or other comment from them. But not a word about my social enterprises was ever expressed. Unlike Jock, before me, it is true that I was a little more discrete in my socialising than he was. In addition, through Mark, who was in the Security Service; and, also because of correspondence I had had with the British Council back in the UK, I did have a dispensation of a sort to join the Iwakuni Culture Society, and even to give talks there. This gave me a ready excuse for meeting and cooperating socially with Japanese people. These personal pursuits of mine must surely have been known to someone in authority. It would have been very interesting to know who in the Security service ever knew of what I was up to; and, if they did, why they had never approached me about them. Needless to say, I was glad that they never did.

Possibility of a hidden hand and protection

It is amusing to assume (although it still remains very much an assumption) that because of my devotion to my tasks I was possibly given some form of protection, or immunity from criticism about my social doings; and this is what gave me the feeling of being "protected". If such were the case, the authority for it could only have come from our Security people and, hence, our AVM. One wonders then just how much AVM Bouchier did possibly know of my social activities and of what I was up to in my spare time. It was just this kind of thinking which latterly led me to my speculating in Chapter 25 that there was possibly far more significance in my visit to General MacArthur's HQ in Tokyo, than I had ever imagined. Certainly, when I went to Tokyo, in the summer of 1946, there were a number of very intriguing co-incidences present in my situation in Iwakuni at that time. They make my musings on the visit interesting, and even plausible. It would follow that, without my knowledge, I may even have been nominated to fill some new or vacant post in the Occupation Forces; and then selected to meet, at that time the most powerful man on earth; but, in the end, I botched it. However, it could also well be that my imagination has been tempted to roam much further than it should; and, in that case, almost anything becomes credible. As to inaction by our Security people, it is of course perfectly possible that the situation in Iwakuni, was so calm and quiet while I was there, that they never had any security problems to bother with at all; and BCAIR's personnel were consequently left to do very much as they wanted.

Mental anguish and simultaneous joys

What is not at all in doubt, especially in the latter days and weeks before I left Japan, is the mental anguish, which I often felt when visiting my Japanese friends, as the anti-fraternisation policy of the Occupation Forces gradually became more effective. I never knew personally of any charges, let alone convictions, being made of Service people for committing a fraternising offence. However, I would, perhaps be out somewhere enjoying the excellent company of my friends, say visiting the cinema or attending a public tea ceremony, or enjoying a pleasant evening with Emiko and the Miyazaki's, and my conscience would immediately step in and spoil the fun. You know you shouldn't really be doing this, don't you? It is against the policy of the Service. It is against the law. Are you being fair to your Organisation? Whatever would your AVM say? To know that what I was doing was strictly against the laws of a service, to which I earnestly wished to be as loyal as I could, was unbearable. It was mental torture. I would wrestle with my mind, pointing out my reasons for doing what I was doing. I had made my friendships when there had been no such laws. They had helped me in my work and had led to many of the successes we had achieved. To break up these friendships now would ruin everything. It was just stupidity to stop. It just didn't make sense. And so I would reason; but, my reasoning was sheer mental torment and painful. The pros and cons of what I was doing would tear away at my mind and sometimes my stomach. It often diverted me from my pursuits and from any thoughts of enjoyment. I am sure that many of the more sensitive and sensible minds of those in authority above us understood the impasse we were in; but the laws remained. I am not sure how matters developed after I left Japan in September 1946 but, as I wrote in chapter 27, I feared that the time for me to leave had come. In my particular case, I may have left, at just about the right time. It all amounted to another important lesson in life to which I have already referred. We always need to be prepared, for our greatest joys to be tempered, sometimes within seconds. Just around the corner from happiness, there may often be great moments of sadness. Fortune frowns as much as it smiles. It is fickle. It is not to be depended on. It is a law which Nature itself tries to teach us; and, invariably, it is also true with manmade laws. It is unfortunate that I should be nearing the end of my writings seemingly on a rather sad note, but it is merely a

Chapter 29: Hard to Believe

lesson in life we all need to learn. It certainly in no way detracts from the value to me of those seven glorious galactic months which I spent in Japan in 1946. Without the shadow of a doubt, they provided me with a truly memorable and valuable experience, which I would not have missed for the world.

CHAPTER 30

AND WHAT CAME NEXT?

Postcript Japan

Taking the country as a whole, Japan worked extremely hard in the years after 1946; and, gradually, if very painstakingly, happily regained its economic strength. With its massive car production and its ingeniously magnificent, hand held, electronic calculators in the 1970's and 1980's especially, Japan dazzled the world. At a personal level, and following my return to the UK in the autumn of 1946, I continued to exchange letters with Emiko for several months. Inevitably, however, our letters became more and more infrequent and we realised that we were on different paths in our lives. We were each seeking our own individuality and permanent future. Emiko married an American officer on duty at the Iwakuni Naval base, which had been HQ BCAIR where I had been stationed, and she then went o to live in Hawaii and started a family. She is still there and we keep in touch by Christmas card, after all these years. As regards Shizue, whom I got to know so well very soon after my arrival in Japan, and who was such a wonderful help to me at the Iwakuni Cultural society, it is only very recently indeed that a present day dear friend of mine, Miharu Takada San, who lives in Tokyo, has very kindly located Shizue's two nieces for me. The elder niece still lives in Iwakuni, while her younger sister is now living in Kanagawa prefecture. Unfortunately, both Shizue and her younger brother Yukiyoshi have now died, but in due course I am still hoping

Chapter 30: And What Came Next?

to resume contact with their family. Returning to !946, for a moment, cards and letters continued to come for a time from Jack Evans, the Australian Newspaper correspondent who had been my roommate in Room 69, and from several girls in the typing pool, but again our letters quickly dwindled in number. To the contrary, Lt. Aizawa, whom I first met in India immediately after the war (as described in Chapter 1), kept in close contact with me until he died just a few years ago. He even claimed to have seen me during my unexpected visit to Tokyo in 1946 (described in chapter 25). My first Christmas card each year, which arrived punctually early in November, was from Lt. Aizawa. He became Captain and Chief Executive of a large Merchant ship belonging to the Nippon Yusen Kaisha. One evening in 1964, when we were both in the United States, I went aboard his ship in New York harbour and was introduced to his crew. We met again during my 3 weeks holiday in Japan in 1990 and, among other ventures, we visited Nikko together. He gave me a copy of a book he had published entitled "Memories of a Second Lieutenant" in which he had mentioned me. During that same holiday, I also went back to Iwakuni; where, even after all the time I had been away, the Iwakuni City offices were still able very kindly to give me the latest addresses of both Fusae San who, previously had been my room girl, and Kamisugi San or "Chiefy", who had been the Iwakuni area's Police Chief. Fusae San, now known as Saguchi San, I was told was living prosperously with her family in Nara. I telephoned and visited her in Nara, and I then spent three very happy days there with her and her family. Within a year she had visited me here in the UK, accompanied by her daughter who was a senior steward with Japanese Airlines, and we have since then also kept in touch every Christmas. As regards former Police chief Kamisugi San, I was told that he now owned a small stationery/newspaper business in Iwakuni and that he was living there with his daughter. Unfortunately, when I called on him, his daughter said that he was not really well enough to talk to me. For me, that was a very sad moment as I would dearly have loved to share a few happy memories with him. I also visited the Iwakuni Naval base mentioned above. The base was still occupied by United States Forces and I was looked after very kindly, for the best part of a day, by an American major. The splendid building which had been HQ BCAIR was still there, but it had been refurbished following an extensive fire. I soon located what had been AVM Bouchier's office, the AOA's office, as well as my own office on the first floor. I also found the room which had been my bedroom at ground level. It was all becoming a very nostalgic visit. I made a point of visiting the Miyazaki's cycle shop, but Emiko's parents, unfortunately by then, had died. Her brother recognised me and he very kindly drove me to the Fukugawa ryokan where Mrs Fukugawa also recognised me. She introduced me to her son who, when I was previously there, had not yet been born. However, he was by now part owner/director of the large famous International Hotel opposite the Kintai bashi, of which I still have the lovely painting described in Chapters 9 and 18. The Aburaya ryokan was still there but the elderly lady in charge didn't recognise me, although I do believe that she was one of the two sisters with whom I used to do so much business.

Postcript the UK

Taking the country as a whole, the UK has now, 66 years on, clearly said good bye to its Empire, which, in 1946, was indeed still very much in existence. This is a change which has come about largely because of the increasing amount of interactive, global developments, which have been going on daily in a rapidly changing world. Fortunately, by working as partners, through thick and thin, with both the Commonwealth and the United States, in the Occupation of Japan in 1946, the UK has still retained much influence in today's world; and, when called upon to do so, is well able to draw on its experience of bygone days. At the personal level, I have less information about my UK acquaintances in Japan in 1946 than I have about my Japanese friends whom I have already mentioned. At the top of my list, I have of course, Air Vice Marshal Bouchier who was appointed very soon afterwards to General MacArthur's inner staff in Tokyo, and who again served with distinction in the Korean War. In his very interesting autobiography "Spitfires in Japan" there is a very moving chapter of his time in Japan. Flt Lt. Cortazzi, whom I mentioned in Chapter 3, became Sir Hugh Cortazzi, a very distinguished writer, especially on Japanese matters, as well as later, becoming British Ambassador to Japan, and then Chairman of the UK Japan Society. The only other UK acquaintance I had in Japan in 1946 about whom I now have information, was my lifetime friend, Mark McLaughlin. After the war, he became a very successful business man in Portugal. He made frequent visits to the UK with his Portuguese wife, Sara, and we met at least once a year. Invariably, when we met, we reminisced at length about our remarkably and memorably happy days in Japan. Sadly, both Mark and his wife died a couple of years ago. I would have greatly appreciated Mark's comments while writing this book; but, unfortunately, I was a year or two, too late. I am, however, sure that if Mark was still here with us, he would have been delighted that I had at last finally put on record a personal account of those many memorable events, in which he too had played a very significant part.

Postscript myself

The seven wonderful months which I spent in Japan in 1946 have had a marked effect on me throughout my life. I joined the UK Foreign Office and I was transferred later to UK HM Treasury. I was extremely busy but, despite many competing pressures, I retained a widening interest in Japan, in its language and its customs, for most of the following 66 years. It was as if my stay in Japan had cast a spell over me and I was continually reminded of its message. You must not forget 1946, and the lessons which it taught you. Hence, since my return to the UK, I have regularly visited SOAS, the School of Oriental Studies in London University where my interest in Japan first began. I became a lifelong member of the Japan Society and several other Japan societies. Among these was Anjinkai (anjin meaning literally, a pilot) which was named after William Adams who is believed to have been the first Englishman to have arrived in Japan in the year 1600, and was the first man to have established trade links between Japan and the UK. This was the society at which during one of its annual festivals, I won my fabulous three weeks holiday in Japan in 1990, to which I have referred at several points in my text. The society unfortunately is no longer with us. Later, I became a member of Sakurakai (Sakura meaning literally cherry blossom) whose meetings I have attended every Tuesday over the last 25 years. In addition, we have in the UK, the Japan Society, the Japanese Embassy, the Japan Foundation, and the Daiwa Corporation. All these splendid bodies, all in London, are continuously and tirelessly organising film shows, book launches, lectures, and many other amazing functions and events to do with Japan. We have much to thank these bodies for, in keeping these fascinating activities alive. However, for me, perhaps even more importantly are the lessons which my experiences taught me about life itself. These lessons are now embedded within me. Maybe they are a little reminiscent of the Boy Scout motto I referred to in my talk to the Iwakini Cultural Society in Chapter 19 that we should always "Be Prepared". We need always to be ready and able to respond to immediate changes in our fortune. All countries, all people, collectively and individually, without any doubt, enjoy and suffer inevitable peaks and troughs, highs and lows, and ups and downs of fortune. We must never be surprised at these sudden changes in fortune. My book, Memoires of Japan 1946 (A People Bowed but not Broken), is a record of how the Japanese people, bravely tackled their own terrible down period of misfortune; and how, amidst all the gloom and despair which followed a ghastly gruesome war, they survived it. They may have been down but they were not out. My account is a tale of those disastrous times of 66 years ago. It is just one story of how wonderfully the Japanese people, at first stoically stood and faced up to their trials; and, then in 1946, very remarkably and commendably, began to overcome them. It was the year in which their first seeds of recovery were sown.

Appendix A

Paragraph Headings By Chapter

Chapter 1:   Kicking Our Heels
  Kashmir, India 3
  Three months in New Delhi 3
  Kindness in India 4
  Goodbye from the Red Fort 5
  Staging Post Madras 5
  Staging Post Bombay 6

Chapter 2:   Bombay to Japan
  Goodbye Bombay 8
  Columbo to Singapore 9
  The South China Seas 10
  Hong Kong, Taiwan, and beyond 11

Chapter 3:   Arrival in Japan
  Historical musings 15
  Shattered dreams 16
  Air Force reception 16
  The harsh reality of Kure 17
  Heartbreak in Hiroshima 18
  Hiroshima's indelible imprint 20

Chapter 4:   Chain of Command
    AMG-BCOF-BCAIR 22
    Arrival in Iwakuni 23
    Feelings sink again 24

Chapter 5:   The Early days
    Air Officer Administration (AOA) 26
    Refurbishing BCAIR HQ 28
    Accommodating HQ staff 29
    A home for the AVM 30
    Privileged guest of the AVM 30
    Sad disposal of swords at sea 31

Chapter 6:   The Namiwaki's—A Glimpse of Family Life
    Mrs Namiwaki, Shizue and her younger brother 33
    Shizue, a girl of hidden talent 34
    Visits and trips along the river 35

Chapter 7:   Daily Routine at the Camp
    Title: Org. 3 36
    Piecemeal build up of our forces 38
    The daily muster of manual labour 39
    Requisitioning 40
    Harrowing experiences 41

Chapter 8:   Appreciation From Girls at the Camp
    Invaluable support for Allied troops 43
    A special show for a departing Squadron 44
    Message from the show and our response 45

Chapter 9:   Party-Going and the Story of A Geisha
    Fugawa Ryokan 47
    Different atmosphere/different participants 48
    Formal introductions 49
    Doomed from childhood 49
    True stories and myths 50
    The impact of War 51
    Mea culpa: 51

Appendix A

Chapter 10:   Happy Days with the Namiwaki's
　　Nothing is forever...53
　　An unexpected Sunday visit...54
　　The Inland Sea at its best...55
　　A splendid catch of fish..55
　　The Namiwaki's at home 56

Chapter 11:   Changing Times
　　Home by Jeep...58
　　Increasing Org. 3 workload 59
　　Visiting VIPs 60
　　Important contacts..61

Chapter 12:   The local Police Chief
　　First encounter 62
　　Difficult decisions 63
　　Chiefy in his office 64
　　Chiefy's District interpreter..65

Chapter 13:   AMG Liaison Officer
　　Mr Kawamura...67
　　At work and socially 68

Chapter 14:   The Mayor
　　Official relationship 69
　　A dubious invitation 70
　　Mayoral dinner 70
　　Different views on Black market activity 71

Chapter 15:   The City Headmaster
　　School curricula overturned..73
　　Iwakuni's School 74
　　Bewilderment..74
　　Allied Forces' interest 75
　　A good intention goes wrong 76
　　Unhelpful actions by Allied Forces 76

- 191 -

Chapter 16: The Miyazaki's—Another Wonderful Family!
- Emiko 78
- An unscheduled visit 79
- Harmony is irresistible 80
- A magical entrance 81
- A typical Japanese room 81
- A new world 83
- The evening's entertainment 84
- Introduction to the "koto" 84
- Unstoppable time 86
- A private talk with Jock 86

Chapter 17: Good Bye To Jock and The End of an Era
- BCAIR's first most valuable asset 103
- No final farewell party 104
- Fraternisation 105
- From rumours to facts 105

Chapter 18: Walkabouts in Iwakuni
- Fortitude in misfortune 107
- A bridge to reality 108
- Beyond the bridge 109
- Main street, Aburaya hotel, and the shops 110
- Evening walks 111
- A typically local discussion 112

Chapter 19: The Iwakuni Cultural Society
- Iwakuni Shin Bunka Domei 114
- Loopholes in the law 115
- Principal members 116
- The committee and the top table. 118
- The status of women 119
- British Youth 120
- Question time 121

Chapter 20: Contact with the Miyazaki's is Resumed
- Effect of Jock's departure 123
- The wanderer returns 124

Appendix A

Animated chatter 125
One of the family..126
Conversation at dinner 127
A little introspection..128
Introducing Peter...129

Chapter 21:   Visit to the Local Mrs Vanderbilt and
              My First Tea Ceremony
Invitation impossible to refuse...130
A remarkable and gracious lady.......................................131
Mrs Fujimoto's home...132
Relaxation 133
Preliminaries 133
Purification...134
Taking our seats 135
Tea Ceremony Par Excellence 136
End of a memorable day...137

Chapter 22:   The Cultural Society and Humour
Absence of humour in our lectures 139
Humour from Scotland 140
Not all humour is amusing 141
Laughing at the loss of personal dignity........................141
Laughing at the obvious 142
Humour from word play and a difference with Emiko 143

Chapter 23:   The Cultural Society and The Status of Women
A perennial topic 145
A living example of inequality...146
A Challenge to Western views...146
Preparations for a talk 147

Chapter 24:   Talk on the Average British Housewife
Main points 149
Freedom of choice...150
Differing customs continue..151
Questions in abundance 152
Alone with my thoughts 153

Chapter 25: An Unexpected Visit To Tokyo
Out of the Blue 154
My job as one time Courier 155
The AVM's Private Jet 156
General MacArthur's HQ 156
A stroll in the Ginza 157
Reflections on the visit 158

Chapter 26: With the Miyazaki's at the Pictures
The danger of taking risks 160
Worries are temporarily overcome 161
The film begins 162
Local customs must be observed 163
Homeward bound 164
End of a fascinating visit 165

Chapter 27: Final Days and Fond Farewells
A time to leave 167
Formal farewells were not possible 168
Individual Goodbyes 168
My last evening with Emiko 170
The last sad morning 171

Chapter 28: A Charmed Existence
Throughout my stay 175
Influence above rank 176
Never once rebuked or criticised 177
Lessons in life 178

Chapter 29: Hard to Believe
No direct control or supervision 180
Possibility of a hidden hand and protection 181
Mental anguish and simultaneous joys 182

Chapter 30: And What Came Next?
Postcript Japan 184
Postcript the UK 186
Postcript myself 187

INDEX

A

Aburaya 109-11, 169, 186
Air Ministry 32, 37
Aizawa 4, 155-6, 185
Aizen katsura 162
Amaterasu 15
American Military Government 22, 31, 41-2, 67-8, 115, 154
Americans 23-4, 76, 80, 164
AMG 22, 25, 37, 67, 154-9, 169
AMG HQ 156
Anjinkai 187
anti-fraternisation 34, 46-7, 58, 61, 84, 115, 157, 161, 168, 178, 180, 182
AOA 7, 26-7, 32, 36-8, 55, 69, 105, 154, 158, 171, 176, 186
"arranged marriage" 149
atom bomb 127
Australia 26, 103, 105
Australians 22, 24, 38, 46, 103
AVM 22, 27-8, 30-2, 36, 59-60, 64, 69, 104, 123, 154, 156, 158-9, 176-7, 181-2, 185

B

Baden Powell 121
barracks 40-1
BCAIR 9, 22, 24, 26-8, 36, 38, 48, 103-4, 118, 157-8, 167, 176-7, 181, 184-5

BCOF 22-3, 31, 37-8, 68, 103, 155
belly button savings 152
black market 17, 71-2, 75, 106, 109, 157
Bofu 37, 44, 59, 79, 87, 103, 114, 123-4, 168, 170
Bolster 30, 48, 60, 64
Bombay 6-10, 26, 109
Bouchier vii, 22, 26, 28, 30, 36-7, 48, 59-60, 69, 104, 123, 154, 158-9, 171, 176-7
Boy Scout motto 188
Boy Scouts 121
British Council 106, 115, 181
British Embassy 156
British Way of Life 106
Buddhist altar 82
Burma 3, 5-6, 23, 115, 176
Butsudan 82

C

calligraphy 56, 77
Captain Brown 169
charmed existence 175, 177-8
Chiefy 62-6, 68-9, 130, 144, 169, 185
Chushingura 78
Columbo 9
Commodore Perry 165
Commonwealth 7, 9, 22-4, 26, 30, 36-7, 53, 115, 186
Cortazzi 37, 186

customs 79, 105, 108-9, 114, 117, 120, 127, 130, 151, 163, 187

D

Dai Ichi 156
daily muster 28, 39, 64, 141
daimyo 4, 163
Daiwa Corporation 187
Dakota 154
Datia 4
democracy 46, 77
diplomats 8, 10, 17, 60
discrimination 151
divorce 150-2

E

earthquakes 179
Education officer 74, 76, 118-20
Emiko 44, 46, 78-9, 81, 83-7, 122-9, 139, 143-4, 147, 155, 160-3, 165, 169-70, 182, 184
equal rights 145-6, 149-50, 152, 159
European dress 160
Europeans 80, 118
eviction 62-3
Exchange rate 30

F

farewell 5, 45, 51, 72, 104, 168, 170
feminine inferiority 126
flower arrangement 56, 135
fraternisation 34, 38, 46-7, 52, 58-9, 61, 77, 84, 105-6, 115-16, 124, 128, 131, 157, 168
fraternising 104-5, 182
free rein 167
fude 56
Fuji San 134-5, 137
Fujimoto 130-8, 171
Fujimura 116-20, 122, 134-5, 137, 169
Fukugawa 47, 51-2, 169, 177, 186
furusato 150

Fusae 29, 142, 166, 171, 185
fusuma 83

G

geisha 47, 49-51, 177
General MacArthur 37, 106, 154, 156-7, 159, 181, 186
ghosts 20
Ginza 157-8
Girl Guides 121
"Go between" 149
golden age of economic prosperity 108
Golden Bridge 47, 108, 111
guard room 169

H

Hank 9, 32, 67, 159
harrowing experiences 41-2
hashi 35
hashira 71
hataraki bachi 108
Hawaii 83, 125, 184
headmaster 73, 116-18, 120, 122, 169
Heso kuri 152
hibachi 83, 124
Hideyoshi 130
Hiroshima 9, 18-24, 45, 113-14, 127, 175, 178
Hiroshima's wounds 113
Hong Kong 11
hospitality 34, 71, 80, 126, 131
housewife 147, 149-50
humoa 141
humour 27, 80, 139-44, 157

I

Ichioka 116
ikebana 56, 135
India 3-6, 10, 26, 37, 103, 105, 144, 155, 176, 185

Index

inequality 146
Inland Sea 15, 32, 55
interpreters 34, 47, 65-6, 169, 176, 179
intriguing coincidences 181
Iwakuni 9, 17-19, 22-4, 32-4, 37-8, 40-1, 47-8, 61-2, 65-7, 73-4, 103-4, 107-8, 113-16, 180-1, 184-5
Iwakuni cinema 160
Iwakuni Cultural Society 34, 73, 114, 123, 168, 176
Iwakuni Golden Bridge 47, 108
Iwakuni Naval base 184-5

J

Jack Evans 29, 113, 171, 185
Janet v, 6
Japan Foundation 187
Japan Society vii, 37, 186-7
Japanese Airlines 185
Japanese characters 10, 16, 57, 77, 139
Japanese culture 114, 116-17
Japanese Embassy vii, 187
Japanese home life 35, 58, 84, 126
Japanese inn 110
Japanese Judas tree 162
Japanese rooms 81
Japanese Tea ceremony 130, 137
Japanese way 115, 127, 170
Japanese women 4, 45, 84, 125, 146, 152
Japan's National Constitution 159
jinrikisha (rickshaws) 158
Jock 27, 33-7, 40-2, 46, 48, 53-9, 61-5, 69-70, 78-81, 83-7, 103-7, 114-17, 123-5, 160, 168-70
Jon, Ken, Pon 64

K

kakejuku 82, 111
kakemono 82, 111
kaki 56

Kamisugi 62, 185
Kanagawa 184
Kanji 16
Kashmir 3
Kawamura 67-8, 115, 169
Kikkawa 30, 60
Kintai bashi 47, 108, 111, 186
ko-gane 43
Kokusai Kanko hotel 47
koto 79, 84-6, 170
Kure 11, 15-18, 20, 22-4, 37-8, 45, 103, 105, 171

L

Lafcadio Hearn 5, 44
legal looting 68
the local dentist 116
local medical doctor 116

M

MacArthur 22-3, 37, 106, 154, 156-7, 159, 181, 186
Madras 5-6, 115
Main Street 110
Manga 142
Mark 6, 115-16, 118, 121, 131-2, 135, 137, 139-42, 169-70, 176-7, 180, 186-7
Mayor 69-70, 169
mental anguish 161, 182
Mess 5, 29, 44, 86, 122-4, 155, 157, 170-1
Mickey 65-6, 116, 130-2, 169
Miho 37
Military Police 51, 177
Miss P 49-51
Mitajiri 23
Miyazaki's 49, 78-84, 107, 109, 122-6, 128-9, 131, 143, 147, 160, 164-5, 169-70, 182, 186
mompei 17
Mrs Fujimoto 130-8, 171
Mrs Miyazaki 86, 125-7, 161-2

Mrs Namiwaki 33, 56
Mrs Vanderbilt 130-1
Mt Fuji 156
Murasaki Shikibu 151

N

"Nakodo San" 149
Namiwaki's 33-4, 49, 53-6, 58-9, 79, 83-4, 107, 131
Nara 185
Nature 15, 106, 128, 179, 182
Naval Air 22, 24
New Delhi 3-6
New Zealand 26, 103, 105, 169
Nikko 185
Nippon Yusen Kaisha 4, 185
Nirvana 126
Nishiki 47, 108, 111
Northcott 22

O

O Cha-no-yu 130
"o-mia" 149
"o mocha" 125
Occupation 28, 34, 38, 40, 51, 60, 83, 105, 115, 128, 132, 141, 145, 156, 180-2
Occupation policy 128
Officers' Mess 44, 155, 157
Okayama 22
Org. 3 27-8, 30-1, 36-7, 59-60, 69, 177
Osaka Shinbun 115

P

Peter 129, 160, 162-5, 170
Picasso 19
Pidgin English 76, 129
Police Chief 62, 185
Police officer 70-2, 122
POWs 4-5, 8, 10
Purse strings 152

R

RAF Regiment 30, 48, 60, 64
realities of life 178
Red Fort 4-5
requisitioning 30, 36, 40-2, 46, 61, 68, 141, 159, 180
Richard Mason 6
rickshaws 158
Robert Browning 161
Room 69 185

S

Saguchi 185
Sakurakai 187
samisen 79, 170
samurai 4, 78, 107, 121, 151, 163-4
sandals 75, 143
Sayonara 146
Scissors, Stone, and Paper 64
Scotland 104, 140, 170
Scottish pronunciation 76
Sen-no-Rikyu 130
Sensei 73-7
sensu 45
Shakespeare 31
Shikoku 22
shiri mochi 142
Shizue 33-5, 37, 53-6, 58, 65, 79, 83-4, 116-20, 122, 139, 147-8, 169, 184
Singapore 9-11, 32, 67
SOAS 3-4, 6, 187
Spitfires in Japan vii, 31, 186
status of women 119, 125, 145
stoicism 17, 80, 178
sumi 56
Sumo wrestling 68
supervision 73, 180
Supreme Allied Commander 159
swords 31, 45, 67

T

Taj Mahal 6
Takada 112-13, 184
takeko 56
tatami 75, 82, 162
teaching syllabus 73
toko-no-ma 71, 82-5, 135
tokobashira 82
Tokyo viii, 9, 22-3, 32-3, 37, 67, 105, 154-9, 178, 181, 184-6
Transport chief 169
tsunamis 179
typhoons 179
typing pool 47, 147, 169, 171, 185

U

UK liaison office 9, 32, 156
United States Army 29, 38

V

VIPs 60, 64
voting rights 151

W

"Wa, Wa-hei, and Wa-go" 80
waraji 143
Western policies 76
Winston Churchill 31
women's suffrage 159
word play 143

Y

Yamaguchi 22, 143-4
Yamisoba 54
Yukiyoshi 33, 35, 55, 184

Printed in Great Britain
by Amazon.co.uk, Ltd.,
Marston Gate.